the
clothes
make
the girl
(look fat)?

DEY ST.
An Imprint of WILLIAM MORROW

the clothes make the girl

(look fat)?

ADVENTURES AND AGONIES IN FASHION

BRITTANY GIBBONS

THE CLOTHES MAKE THE GIRL (LOOK FAT)?. Copyright © 2017 by Brittany Gibbons. All rights reserved. Printed in the United States of America. No part of this book may be used or reproduced in any manner whatsoever without written permission except in the case of brief quotations embodied in critical articles and reviews. For information, address HarperCollins Publishers, 195 Broadway, New York, NY 10007.

HarperCollins books may be purchased for educational, business, or sales promotional use. For information, please email the Special Markets Department at SPsales@harpercollins.com.

FIRST EDITION

Designed by Paula Russell Szafranski

Interior art © Sviatlana Sheina/Shutterstock

Library of Congress Cataloging-in-Publication Data has been applied for.

ISBN 978-0-06-249923-3

17 18 19 20 21   DIX/LSC   10 9 8 7 6 5 4 3 2 1

This book is dedicated to my daughter, who changes her clothes every half hour. Never stop trying things on, Gigi. I love you from your toes to the top of your laundry pile.

CONTENTS

PROLOGUE

There is a certain level of hypocrisy in writing this fashion memoir while I'm sitting at my desk dressed like Winnie-the-Pooh.

You know, naked from the waist down while wearing a crop top.

But the truth is, even Anna Wintour isn't dressed like Anna Wintour all the time. On her days off from *Vogue,* she's probably feet up in a La-Z-Boy wearing leggings as pants and the free sweatshirt she got for signing up for a Capital One card in college.

I'm still paying off that card, too, Anna. I see you.

Now, before we get too far into things, I realize that some of you may be holding this book in your hands with absolutely no idea who I am. Maybe you bought it because the cover was cute, or someone left it in the bathroom of a bar, or your one passive-aggressive aunt thinks it's a weight-loss book and gave it to you with well-intentioned concern about your health. However you got it, hello. My name is Brittany Gibbons. My first memoir, *Fat Girl Walking*, is a *New York Times* best seller, and I became famous for being a fat woman who takes her clothes off to make others feel less bad about their bodies.

I started blogging in 2007, which is something frustrated writers do while they are waiting to publish their first novel.

"She's just writing on the Internet until she finishes her book," my mom assured everyone in the grocery store each week.

I began and failed as a food blogger, and then went on to build a half-million-per-month readership on my website, *Brittany Herself,* by chronicling my painfully honest body-acceptance journey. What started as something I did in front of a computer screen in my bedroom at 3 A.M. with a baby on my breast and another in the crib beside me, something born out of loneliness and insomnia and self-hate, has turned into a decade-long career often out of reach for someone living in a small town in Ohio. What follows is the weirdest résumé, ever.

SPOKESMODEL

The first time a major fashion brand reached out to me, it was done with a one-line cold-call e-mail in my in-box.

I work with a major fashion brand who'd love to speak to you; I'd love to connect you!

I was writing with an amazing group of women at the time on an online e-zine called *Curvy Girl Guide,* a website I'd thought of while brushing my teeth and wondering what my thick legs would look like in tall leather boots and feeling frustrated I couldn't find any pictures of women like me online. I answered that e-mail, which very much could have been some sort of Nigerian lottery scam, and was connected with my first real fashion brand, Lands' End. After creating two amazing swimsuit confidence campaigns with them through *Curvy Girl Guide,* I was signed to a solo fashion campaign to help them relaunch their plus-size line. It was through them that I cut my fashion teeth. I've gone on to work with many other fashion brands, some completely new to the plus-size space, and others that have been doing plus for a while, and are just finally ready to say the word out loud. I curate collections, I advise on seasonal lines, and I work as a spokesmodel, often appearing in catalogs and in online marketing.

I've made a conscious effort to work only with brands that I would not only wear, myself, but that were actually affordable and accessible to real, everyday women. Women who, like me, didn't invent Facebook and often financially put themselves last. I want to make that prioritization an easier step, and working with clothing brands that are within budget helps me convince you to do just that.

MAKEOVER QUEEN

I've spent a huge amount of time watching fashion make-over shows on television. *What Not to Wear, How Do I Look?, A Makeover Story, Ten Years Younger, Extreme Makeover, The Swan, Revenge Body* . . . you get the picture. What all of the shows have in common is that they come with a healthy dose of shame. *Ten Years Younger* used to put the subjects in a clear booth and make strangers on the street guess their age, and *How Do I Look?* would gather all of your friends and let them trash your wardrobe in front of you. I've sat Andy down on the couch, crouched down to his level, and told him in no uncertain terms that if he ever took me on one of those shows and they tried to take away my gray sweatpants with the hole in the crotch, I would burn the studio down and divorce him so hard he'd have to join a monastery to find purpose again.

What Not to Wear was actually pretty fantastic in that Stacey and Clinton were not only insanely knowledgeable about fit and fashion, they were also extremely compassion-ate. However, can I just say, thank God I was never on that show because that secret footage they take of you before you know you're getting a makeover would just be endless blurry black-and-white Big Foot–like film of me singing Hall & Oates in my car or stopping at every sample table at Costco on a Saturday.

Shame aside, one of the bigger issues of these shows was that when it came to plus-size bodies, nobody really knew what to do with them, so instead they focused on ways to teach them to minimize themselves enough that they could wear the largest size they could find in a store, and hope for the best.

First, most fat women don't get the luxury of shopping in a real store, all our shit has to be ordered online, a Jesus candle lit when it ships, and then tried on in an empty dark bedroom with the air conditioner blasting to fifty degrees. We all know this. Second, you're assuming any of us know how to dress ourselves, and some switch is magically going to flip back on inside us like, duh, I guess I do like belts to hit at my natural waist.

People, no. We don't have a style because we've never really had the option to develop a style. We've developed coping mechanisms ... there's a difference. Plus-size women are just now learning what straight-size women figured out in high school. We never got to be the princess, we never got to be the cheerleader, we never even got to be the Manic Pixie Dream Girl. We simply didn't have access to the supplies.

We have spent decades being ignored by the fashion industry, so I now spend a lot of time helping women figure out how to make plus-size clothing work for them, and I do it by surprising them with head-to-toe makeovers. We spend the day together, I help them discover their style, I come armed with piles of clothes sent from amazing plus-size brands that support me, and it's truly the most empowering thing I do. Like, Tammy-Faye-Bakker-mascara-running-down-my-face empowering.

CHUBBY MEDIA DARLING

As a rule, I don't watch myself on television. I might love my body and be really, really proud of the work that I do, but I'm still a woman and I know my triggers. Watching my interviews and appearances would negate all the good feelings I had about the experience, and instead I'd focus on some sort of physical flaw or weird thing my hair was doing.

So I choose to abstain, but I do love getting my work out there, whether it be in glossy magazines or on talk shows. I am brought on to speak out about body shaming and the bullying of both teens and adults, as well as to offer fun plus-size fashion insight. Seeing these segments become more regular, and seeing them not treat body love and the struggle to achieve it like a trend is huge, but it wasn't always that easy to get people to pay attention.

I've resorted to some pretty provocative means to get my message across. I've stripped onstage during a TED Talk. I have stood in Times Square in my bathing suit, twice. I've walked around a bookstore in New York in a pair of see-through panties. There are literally more pictures of me on the Internet without clothes than with. And I faintly remember that long ago there was a woman who existed in a three-bedroom house in Delta, Ohio, who cried every night over her three sleeping babies because she wasn't sure she deserved them, or that they'd ever want to be seen with her in public when she could barely stand catching her own reflection in the glass door of the supermarket. But I don't know that woman anymore.

ADULT SUMMER CAMP OWNER
(NO, FOR REAL)

You know what's hard? Making friends as an adult. Everyone always talks about how hard it is for kids to make
friends, but they never consider how miserable the experience is for grown-ups. With the exception of two lifelong
friends, I don't really keep in touch with the people I went
to high school with, even though I'm living in my hometown. Connections in college never quite took. That leaves
coworkers and the adults you're put into contact with because of your kids. Sometimes that totally works out, but
other times it doesn't.

There are very few things as painful as trying to make a
one-way adult friendship happen, believe me.

Five years ago I put that need for camaraderie, all the
knowledge I'd picked up working at a summer camp after
college, as well as growing up watching marathons of *Meat-
balls, Indian Summer, Camp Nowhere,* and *Wet, Hot American
Summer,* and I created Camp Throwback. Camp Throwback is a weeklong nostalgic summer camp for adults. It
has all the fun of adolescence, like friendship bracelets,
field day, slip 'n' slides, and parties, but with all the perks
of adulthood, like booze. It's also a really chill place where
adults can go to fit in, meet cool people, and give absolutely
no fucks walking around the pool in a bathing suit. I get to
run this camp with a clipboard, megaphone, and knee-high
tube socks every summer.

Andy calls it my "precommune." And he's not wrong. I
told him when he married me that if I was ever presented

with a chance to live in a commune, I would take it. And I don't mean the off-the-grid religion- or politics-based communes. Mass suicide is not a good look on me.

I just want to live in the middle of nowhere on a big plot of land with a group of like-minded individuals so that we can grow some food, French-braid each other's hair, raise our kids together like a village, and have our cycles align so we can all eat carbs and drink wine together on the couch watching *Orange Is the New Black*. The whole group-sex aspect would be entirely optional. Oh, and we'd probably have some chickens or whatever.

DIGITAL SORORITY HOUSE MOTHER

Curvy Girl Guide began as an online magazine in 2010, with a staff of over twenty writers, headed by myself and my friend Heather Spohr. As the online climate evolved, and editors and writers came and went, running it in its then-current form became ineffective. As in, we weren't as effective as we needed to be, and became just another place for curated magazine content trying to keep up with other curated and regurgitated online magazine content. The race for shares and clicks and platform was exhausting. The nail in the coffin of the magazine came when I was sued by a huge photo service because a writer used a picture of Bryce Dallas Howard, a new mom out with her new baby, in an article railing against the shaming of postpartum bodies. *We* hadn't paid for the photo *they* didn't have permission to take. I paid the fines and soon after closed the magazine chapter of Curvy Girl, and looked around the Internet for ways to make real, actual change in the relationships women were having with themselves.

I relaunched *Curvy Girl Guide* as a digital community in 2013. What began as a few hundred women sharing their lives has blossomed into thousands of women from around the globe. Our sisters host local meet-ups, provide 24/7 support, and are made up of every size of the body spectrum. Body image is a women's issue, not just a fat women's issue.

TOTALLY NORMAL PERSON

Lastly, there's my personal life. I am married to Andy, my high school sweetheart, and we have three children: Jude (eleven), Wyatt (ten), and Gigi (eight). And for a long time, I thought that's all there would be for me. I would graduate high school, maybe college, and get married, have kids, and lose myself to that life.

Not that there's anything wrong with that. Being a mom and wife are two strong-ass things that strong-ass women do every day. It's just that I thought I'd be able to hide behind it, to make sure the best parts of me were other people.

Don't pay attention to the insecure woman behind the curtain. Here, look at these kids with cute clothes and trendy haircuts, instead!

Girls like me, from small farm towns in the Midwest . . . we don't grow up to have these sorts of careers. In fact, on my first real job interview after college, I was asked by the HR director where I saw myself in five years.

"Hopefully staying home with my four kids and living near my parents."

I cringe thinking about that. I mean, who tells the person you want to hire you that your goal is to be unemployed?

I never saw this life for me.

I never saw this life for me.

I never saw this life for me, but here we are.

I am a blogger-turned-women's-advocate who writes really graphically about sex, love, food, and my body, and I have an unchecked addiction to helping real women feel good in their skin and the clothes they put on it. And by real women, I mean two things:

1. Humans who identify as women.
2. Women who have to shop on a real budget while also facing real-life obstacles, like work, kids, college, heartbreak, and the general ups and downs of life.

Real women, for the record, are not defined by their curves, thigh gaps, or chest size. Those are just things generally used to make us feel bad about ourselves and have nothing to do with our label or worth as women. It can be confusing, I know. Now back to real woman problems.

Carving out "you time" when you are working sixty hours a week, or swimming in children, or under school deadlines, or suffering from anxiety or depression isn't a reality for many women. It's no wonder we feel terrible about ourselves . . . who has time for self-care when life is kicking our ass?

I am hyperaware that getting free clothes sent to me and then showing them off on Instagram isn't going to help anyone feel better about themselves, per se. It's like watching a lifeboat of plus-size models in Chanel row by while I'm clinging to a piece of wood in an ill-fitting romper from Forever 21. Fifty percent inspiring and 50 percent utterly useless.

What good is clothing inspiration if you can't afford it and don't feel like you are worth dressing or spending money on?

It's important to me to show you how to make things work in a way that is attainable, affordable, and practical to the life of the average woman, a woman, in my opinion, who needs to learn how to be a whole lot kinder to herself. Because that is what I am, an average woman who buys her shoes at Target, only recently started spending more on bras than on wine, and is meanest to herself.

If it feels like a struggle, that is because it absolutely is. Oh my gosh, this book already sounds like such a downer . . . stay with me. My first book was a humorous memoir chronicling my life as a fat girl, from my childhood to the present. It was candid and painful and funny and obscene—all my best adjectives, really. While the book was met with a huge amount of praise, the negative reviews I received came from a point of view I didn't expect.

You see, some people were upset that my book wasn't a

how-to manual for learning to like yourself, and they were even more upset, by the end of it, to learn that I actually didn't always like myself.

Women, we cannot always bullet-point our way into self-love.

I am not sure where we fell into this creepy comfortability with digesting self-help books as a guaranteed way to solve our problems, but if you pick up a book that promises to have you loving yourself 100 percent of the time by the end of it, set it down and light your money on fire. Or give it to orphans, whatever, just let it do something positive in this world instead of having it go toward a complete and utter scam.

Because that is what the promise of constant high self-esteem is: a scam.

Now, what I *can* promise you in this book is an honest account of the things that totally worked for me, the things that I failed miserably at, and the swear-to-God truth that some days I still hate my body. Of course those days are still there; the days when I sob in my closet, and hate all my clothes, and eat because it feels really fucking good to eat. The good news, though, is that those days are fewer and fewer, and when I do have them, it's not a complete system shutdown anymore. It's just a normal part of being a woman, and it's important that you know that. Everybody has those days. *Beyoncé* has those days.

So how do beauty and fashion fit into all of this? Well, on the surface, it seems pretty frivolous and superficial; like

I'm just here feeding into society's beauty standards. First of all, don't let anyone ever make you feel bad for liking clothes and doing your hair and wearing makeup. You are allowed to enjoy yourself in this life, so you do you. Second, a great amount of self-confidence and strength can come from fashion.

If an amazing dress is the motivation that moves you from lying in bed to leaving the house for a night out with friends, you find that dress and you go live.

How do you find that dress? That's what I am here for. To help you figure out what makes you feel the most like you, and how to navigate your way there.

As plus-size women, we find it hard to buy the right clothes because we don't know how to categorize our bodies. We're really only given one of two narratives for them; squat with cumbersome boobs or Amazonian and wide. This is a promise of guaranteed failure because "plus size" isn't one body type.

A little louder for the designers in the back: Plus. Size. Isn't. One. Body. Type.

Plus-size women, like all women, come in a variety of shapes. Some of us have long legs, some of us are petite. Not all of us have a rack like a *Playboy* model, and some of us have boobs for days. We are part of the wide spectrum of women's bodies that are unique and different and unable to fit into the cliché body-type boxes provided to us.

We've all heard of the basics; hourglass, apple, pear, rectangle . . . I find these to be mostly off base, and don't know a single person who qualifies wholly as any of them. I have a friend who's shaped exactly like a dildo—just, like, a huge head then two big kneecaps. Jean shopping is a nightmare.

I, myself, have what I like to call a two-burrito body type. You know, the type of body you have when you've mistakenly eaten two burritos instead of one and as a result you have to unzip your pants and take your rings off when you get back into the car. It really works to my advantage on public transportation, sometimes allowing me to pass for around four months pregnant, always securing me a good seat. All I have to do is rub my tummy and stare wistfully out a window, like maybe I'm dreaming of my future baby, when the reality is, I'm Lamaze-breathing through that extra scoop of guacamole.

If I was in charge of coming up with body types, they'd all come with a big huge asterisk. As in, *Note:* It's totally okay if none of these apply to you, there is nothing wrong with your body, go buy those skinny jeans you tried on earlier.

They'd also feature much more relatable illustrations. Like my friend Jordan who is reverse Hobbit shaped, tiny but with even tinier feet. She always has the cutest shoes, but as a size 11, I can borrow none of them.

My friend Jenn has what she likes to call Once-Used Sleeping Bag body. She's had two C-sections, so she often feels she has to tuck some of her loose tummy skin into her pants, but it never quite fits right. Like trying to get a sleeping bag back into the bag it came in before eventually giving up and just tying a rope around it.

There's Rorschach Test Body, which is something I've noticed in many of my friends who have had gastric bypasses. We all see them walking around in a whole new body, but they see something completely different and their brain still dresses them like they didn't just lose 110 pounds.

FLOTUS arms, which is totally self-explanatory because, damn.

You get the idea. We aren't just fruit. Expecting clothes to fit us one of seven standard ways is a ridiculous concept. Instead, our job is to see what's being produced, have fun with what works for our bodies, discard what doesn't, and certainly never feel bad in the process.

So what is the point of this book? It's not just some book filled with vomited tips and tricks. Not only would that be insanely boring to read, but in a hundred years, when the alien overlords check it out of the library, crop tops and harem pants might not even be a thing.

I'm here to tell you why loving your body is hard and sucks for everyone, regardless of size. And I'll bring you along on my journey of finding my personal style and my quest to live a life outside of maternity underwear and men's undershirts.

We'll talk about all the cringe-worthy things we should be talking about. Like, yes, you can have sex through that Spanx hole. And no, you should not cut your bangs yourself; I don't care how much you've had to drink.

We'll cover personal style, wardrobe malfunctions, and mom bodies. To some body-love veterans, some of the things we talk about in this book might sound insecure, and they are. But that is exactly what so many still feel. This book is for the people who aren't there yet, and there's nothing wrong with that. It's a journey, and it's not my job to brag about how much I love my size and not share how I got here, how I *struggled* to get here, how I'm *still* getting here.

This book is a memoir. It's an overdue love letter to my body. It's a time machine of hilarity and humiliation and who wore it best. It's an angry rant and an empowered battle cry.

It's a movement. Rage on.

INTRODUCTION

"If it doesn't fit, just take it off."

"And then wear what?" I spat, red and sobbing, my face in my hands.

The clear plastic bag the polyester Cleopatra costume came in was on the bathroom counter in front of me, the gold Velcro wristbands and crown completely forgotten as I desperately tried to zip the Egyptian gown around my irritated back fat.

Andy was finishing up the last few elements of his Julius Caesar costume, even once complaining under his breath that the adult large was a touch too big in the waist.

His funeral will be lovely, I thought, *a modest gathering of all of his friends and family.* I'd even spring for a buffet lunch after the service, not just an assortment of hors d'oeuvres.

I had received a last-minute invitation to a coworker's Halloween party and purchased the costumes from a pop-up Halloween store housed in a shuttered Circuit City. The theme was famous couples, and having just had a baby (two years ago), I opted for the most tent-like option.

The plus-size sticker on the bag was deceiving. This dress wasn't an American plus size . . . the kind of plus size that comes from stress, depression, and McRibs. It was the kind of plus size that comes from China, where a 5X is a U.S. size 8.

Andy stepped behind me to take over as my sweaty fingers began to slip from the metal zipper. My flesh was provoked to the point of anger, red and swelling. I had become a human puffer fish.

"If it doesn't fit, just take it off." The nurse buzzed around me, squirting lines of clear jellies on the folded paper towel on the metal tray beside the examination table.

I pulled at the paper robe she'd asked me to change into after removing all my clothing. The folded seam under my right arm split loudly as I tugged the open front sides closer together.

"And just sit here naked?" I asked.

At the time, I had no idea that sitting naked on a table

awaiting my first gynecological exam was the least of the indecencies I would be subjected to in my life as a woman. But as a sixteen-year-old kid, the thought mortified me.

"Mmm-hmm." Beth smiled before leaving the room.

Beth had been my nurse my whole life. She'd taken my rectal temperature as a baby, given me stickers after my kindergarten vaccines, and could tell you, without looking at my medical history, how many ear infections I'd had in my lifetime.

She was also the one who answered the phone when I'd called to tell her I wanted to get on birth control my junior year of high school.

"You know," I nonchalantly said into the phone, "for acne or whatever."

It never occurred to me at the time that getting on birth control would be any different from calling for something to treat a sore throat. When I'd brought the idea up to my mom, she was surprised but the practical liberal inside her nodded and agreed it was probably a good idea. We noted that birth control would be smart to help with cramps and pimples, both of us willing to ignore the fact that my skin was perfectly clear and I was going with the Spanish Club to Mexico in a few months with my boyfriend and limited chaperones.

"You'll have to make an appointment with Dr. Ernie for your first Pap smear."

I'm sorry, what? The first ten years of my life, Dr. Ernie came into the room wearing a clown nose. And now I'm

sitting on the table in an exam room I've never been in before at the end of the hall. These were the rooms reserved
for the grown-ups. Unlike the children's room with colorful wallpaper borders and buckets of germ-covered Duplo
Blocks on the floor, the adult exam rooms were large, with
burgundy paisley wallpaper and racks of pamphlets about
diabetic foot care and colonoscopies.

I was sitting on the table in a too-small paper gown I
wore like a cape, shifting from side to side not only because
I was terrified to leave a wet mark where I sat on the paper
liner, but also because that morning, in a fit of insecurity
about what my vagina might smell like, I'd sprayed myself
with Bath & Body Works Cucumber Melon perfume.

Because that is what insecure teenagers do. They spray
their pubic hair with body spray and hope the gown fits.

"If it doesn't fit, just take it off."

I sat on the very edge of the couch as naturally as possible. If I kept my back completely straight and only exhaled
half of my lung capacity, the dress totally fit.

"I don't understand why you borrowed this dress." My
mom sighed. "It doesn't even fit."

"It fits when I stand up," I argued.

It was a dance, nobody sits at a dance, I think? Honestly,
I had no idea. This was the first time the sisters at my small
Catholic school had thrown a dance for the sixth through

eighth graders, inviting all the area schools to join in from 7 to 9 P.M. on a Friday night. Prior to this event, my social interactions were mostly limited to the eight other kids in my class and the three girls in my Girl Scout troop.

I had borrowed a dress from my best friend Laura's older sister. It was a teal-and-white plaid shift dress with thick straps. The straight fit conflicted with my shape. The neckline puckered from the pull of the folds of my chest, ill supported and shaped in the flimsy bralette I'd insisted on wearing to avoid the giant cupped underwire monsters my mother wore, and the dress barely zipped. My mom quickly added a hook and eye above the zipper for extra hold, just in case.

When I arrived at the school, I quickly removed the salmon-colored cardigan my mom insisted complemented the dress, and walked into the partially dim gym to find only Laura and myself had dressed up for the event. Our normally empty cement-walled gymnasium was now full of public school kids wearing jeans and striped polo shirts that were tucked in only in the front.

No one was dancing; instead they just globbed together in groups. The boys were telling stories with their hands, stopping every few minutes to shake the hair out of their eyes like the characters did on the Nickelodeon shows I watched like *Hey Dude* and *Clarissa Explains It All*. All the girls wore penny loafers without socks and had their bangs clipped back from their faces as they laughed at the boys, playfully batting at their arms in fake disgust.

Laura and a few of my classmates found their own table to gather around and I stood next to them, shaking off any requests to join them as they sat down.

"No thanks, I've been sitting all day," I explained. "It feels good to stand."

I used the sweat from my hands to work my permed bangs to the side. Every so often I saw a boy and girl I didn't know sneak into one of the restrooms for a few minutes before bursting out red-faced and giggling.

I crossed my arms across the front of my stomach, hiding the visible waist of my underwear sitting a few inches above my belly button, and sighed shallowly.

Who needs to expel carbon dioxide from their bodies? I thought. Screw the trees.

"If it doesn't fit, just take it off." My grandma smiled warmly, helping me pull the dress off over my head.

She and my grandfather had returned from a trip visiting my aunt overseas with gifts for me and my brother: chocolates, wooden shoes, a T-shirt from the gift shop near the Eiffel Tower for my brother, Adam, and for me, a beautiful tiered party dress from Paris like I'd seen once in an *American Girl* book.

"Not everything is going to fit you, Brittany," she consoled me. "No shame in taking it off and trying something different."

And just like that, she shook off the matter, giving me the green plaid Scottish shawl she'd brought home for a friend, and blamed the small dress on "crazy European sizing."

It was easy for her not to give the moment a second thought. Jeanne Erausquin, my grandmother, was stunning; slim with long legs and fingers weighted down by rows of costume jewelry. She and her equally beautiful sister, Betty, owned a bridal salon in Toledo, Ohio, and I spent a great deal of time there watching women who looked like them spend money on gorgeous dresses that very much adhered to "European sizing."

What I didn't know at the time was that Jeanne was preparing me for womanhood in a way that no other person had been able to . . . it just took me thirty years to figure this out.

Up until that point, I had perfected a lifestyle of not fitting into things; from clothing, to high school, to the occasional mom clique. But let's be real, sometimes those bitches are crazy.

Wearing something that didn't fit was, surprisingly, an appealing alterative to the otherwise terrible reality of being a fat person in the eighties, nineties, and two thousands. And I'm not talking about the body shaming and stigma. Truthfully, most of that didn't really spread as violently as it did after the Internet happened. Don't get me wrong, people still called you fat, but then you went home and, assuming your family members weren't a bunch of assholes, you got a bit of a break from the hate and were left to try to piece together some semblance of healing quietly on your own.

No, I'm talking about how terrible it was to dress yourself as a fat person back then. Right now, we're living in a plus-size fashion renaissance, but these choices weren't available to me even ten short years ago.

Back then, plus-size fashion was designed and sold to two main demographics: women over sixty and rampant Looney Tunes fans. I don't have the actual statistics, but I feel confident enough to say that roughly 50 percent of plus-size clothing in the nineties featured a bedazzled Looney Tunes character. Now, if the majority of women in this country were and are plus size, and I have yet to come across any sizable petition to bring Bugs Bunny back on the air, wouldn't it be just good business sense to stop putting fucking Tweety Bird on a T-shirt?

It makes me think that designers don't see plus-size women as mature or as fashionable as their skinnier counterparts. We also hold jobs, we go out with friends, and we date. We do normal human activities and feel a healthy desire to do them in clothes that make us feel confident and beautiful and and are reflective of our personalities. Did Gisele Bundchen have to go on her first high school date wearing a T-shirt that said YOU'RE DETHPICABLE? No . . . but I did.

It wasn't until my junior year of college that I shopped at a legitimate plus-size-specific store. Prior to that, the

majority of my wardrobe was made up of youthful clothing that simply didn't fit properly, or matronly clothing my
mother and I purchased from the women's sections of department stores.

My parents were hard-core Sears shoppers, mainly because we were very poor and anyone could get a Sears
credit card. Whenever I needed new clothes, my mom and
I would make the forty-five-minute drive to Sears, hand the
woman at the service desk a piece of paper with my mom's
account number written on it, pay whatever late fees she
had, and then head over to the adult women's section to
peruse their selection of denim pants and Empire-waist
dresses.

I was lucky in that I went to a Catholic school that required a uniform, but my out-of-school clothes left a lot to
be desired, and I often dressed much older than I was, and
I don't mean in the trashy fun way. There is nothing provocative and sexy about elastic slacks.

Fashion became more of a problem once I hit high
school, and transferred from a small private elementary school where nobody cared what you looked like to
a public school where everybody cared what you looked
like. The majority of the clothing I wore in high school
was either completely homemade or purchased on sale and
altered by my mom, a skilled seamstress.

Sewing is a skill I long to pick up but don't have the
patience to acquire. My mom, having altered her share of
dresses at my grandmother's shop, was brilliant with a pat-

tern. Despite this talent, I always grew frustrated that she didn't place the same level of importance on fashion that I did. She's told me often that the last day she wore heels was on her wedding day. Prior to that, she lived a different life as a fancy buyer for a bridal salon, traveling to Chicago and New York monthly. Then she had kids, cut off her waist-length black hair, gave all that up, and now lives in jean shorts and T-shirts with pugs on them.

At the height of nineties grunge, I spent hours trying to find the perfect baby-doll dress to wear to a state choir contest. My mother and I flipped through the McCall's and Simplicity pattern books on the table at Joann Fabrics, only to come up empty. Aprons or housedresses, yes, but apparently Courtney Love chic had not yet hit the do-it-yourself circuit.

On a hunch, my mom took me to the maternity section of JCPenney and selected the longest tunic she could find. It was dark blue with tiny pale blue flowers, cap sleeves, and a detachable elastic clip you could use to cinch the back. It was a hideous shirt to sic on a pregnant person, but on me, a fourteen-year-old girl, if you looked at it just right, it had the same shape as the baby-doll dress in the picture from the dELiA*s catalog that I'd carried with me into every shop that day.

The dress was short and the front was just a touch longer than the back, I assume to accommodate an actual pregnant stomach, but with opaque black tights and knockoff Dr. Martens . . . as long as I didn't bend over, no one was the wiser. From that moment on, women's maternity clothing became a fixture in my high school wardrobe.

While home from college over Christmas break, Andy, whom I was only dating at the time, surprised me with a weekend getaway to a bed-and-breakfast in Upstate New York. Convinced he would be proposing to me on this trip (he did not), I went shopping for all new winter clothes, as well as some sexy lingerie.

I went shopping with my friend Amanda, who was way more self-confident than I, and had no qualms about walking into Lane Bryant to shop.

"This is a fat-lady store," I whispered.

"I'm a fat lady sometimes," Amanda whispered back, and smiled before disappearing into the racks of clothing.

This shopping trip changed my life. For the first time ever, I was picking up trendy clothing in my actual size, taking it to a fitting room, and trying it on without worrying if I'd be able to let the sides out or add fabric so that it would zip.

I bought a long denim skirt with a front slit down the middle, an oatmeal-colored fitted sweater, and a black see-through nightgown.

My trip to Upstate New York did not yield an engagement ring, but it did solidify a few new important things in my life. First, there's the realization that I do not like bed-and-breakfasts. They sound romantic, and look really good on paper, but the reality is that you are renting a room in a house full of other people that you have to eat breakfast next to and pretend that you don't hear having sex or pooping.

The second thing I learned, not only in that stall in Lane Bryant, but also from Andy, who complimented my clothing repeatedly throughout the trip, was that it's better to actually fit into something than to try to squeeze into something that doesn't fit. That sounds like a no-brainer. But the societal conditioning is strong with this one. In my head, it was more important to me to wear Gap jeans that I had to close with a rubber band looped through the buttonhole than it was to go to a legitimate plus-size boutique and buy the same trendy jeans in a larger size.

This is a really hard habit to break, especially when the people that you go shopping with are smaller than you. Fear of Missing Out is a real thing, and not being included in the shopping experience sucks. Take it from me, the girl stuck looking at the candles and dishes at Anthropologie. But eventually you just get to the point where you're tired of the tight zippers and overstuffed bras and standing in a group of people who are having fun, and being so lost in your own head hating your body and what you put on it that you explode. And you explode so hard that you either give up and disappear or you scream, "Not today, Satan," to the girls working inside Victoria's Secret and you walk into the plus-size section of a Target and grab fistfuls of clothes and head into that dressing room determined not to come out until you have something, anything, that lets you feel like a normal human woman who is not consumed with hating herself.

I still explode once or twice a month. I get cocky and order something online whose posted measurements clearly assure me will not fit, but I'm an addict. I can't walk away. And it comes, and it's tight, and I peel it back off of me and lie on the ground hot and sweaty and disappointed in myself.

So I go to Torrid and shut myself in a dressing room in order to remember that I am not those tiny jeans on the floor of my bedroom. I am a normal being with a body that fits into some things and not into others. The fitting room becomes a confessional, and I breathe in and out, trying on my different penances.

"Everything okay in there?" The associate with the thick pink glasses and beautiful tattoo sleeve around her right arm knocked lightly on the door. "How's that bathing suit you brought in there?"

"It doesn't fit, I'm taking it off," I said from inside the changing room. "Can I get a larger size?"

CHAPTER 1

They Found My Body in a Gap Fitting Room

My first real job was at the Gap.

Prior to that, I'd worked as a cashier at a pet store, a hostess at a Mexican cantina, and was a waitress for one day at my family's favorite local Chinese restaurant, but simply didn't have the balance or composure to serve hot bowls of soup on tiny glass plates.

The Gap in the late nineties and early two thousands was a really cool place to be. It was all colorful sweaters, chunky scarves and mittens, and Rent soundtracks. It was truly a new dawn for a brand that had previously been the hub of basic.

Getting hired at the Gap had become a personal goal. My friend Kristin had gotten a job there our senior year of high school, and she always bought the best clothes at a huge discount. Who knows why certain ambitions consume us, they just do. I once spent a whole year trying to write music like Violet in *Coyote Ugly*, but I can't play any instruments and am a terrible rhymer. The heart wants what the heart wants.

Working at the Gap became my unstoppable mission. The basic formula for being hired was as follows:

1. Fill out an application.
2. Wait to be contacted for a cattle-call group interview.
3. Try to out-Gap, outdress, and out-aloof-cool-girl everyone else at the interview.
4. Leave and hope you get called for a one-on-one interview with the managers.

The first group interview I attended I was woefully unprepared for. To start, I wasn't wearing anything from the Gap, which seems like a no-brainer, except that I couldn't really fit into anything from the Gap. I was literally applying to work someplace where the only thing I could comfortably squeeze into was the dressing room. Then I made the grave mistake of trying to befriend the other candidates in the break room before the interview. This is a thing I often do out of blind insecurity; disarming the people around me by telling them they are really pretty, with them accepting the compliment but not returning it, then me trying to entertain them with humor for the remainder of our awkward time together.

Lastly, I was completely uneducated about the brand and what they had to offer. What was my favorite style of jeans? How did I feel about chinos? What were some great register add-ons to offer customers as they checked out? The truth was, I had no idea. I'd barely shopped there.

I did not get a callback for a second interview, but I remained undeterred. I spent the next month going into the store every week, studying their clothes, and trying to piece together the perfect outfit for my next interview attempt.

The Christmas-seasonal-employment group interview was twice the size of the summer one I had attended, but this time I was totally ready. I wore a Gap oversized men's oatmeal cable-knit sweater over a non-Gap denim miniskirt, gray wool tights, and brown matte platform loafers from Bakers Shoes.

Due to the size of the group, the questions were a bit vaguer and more rapid-fire. I assume they needed all hands on deck for the holiday shopping rush, so the barrier to entry had been slightly lowered to: Can you fold clothes? Will you not rob us? A week later I got the callback, had a one-on-one interview, and was hired on the spot.

My mom took me out to celebrate the same way people celebrate when they are accepted into their first-choice college or get engaged. I had just been hired for temporary seasonal employment, but in my head it was a huge cool-girl feat, and my life had been largely bereft of cool-girl feats.

I was imagining working at the Gap to hold the same kind of mysterious cachet that made people envy flight attendants in the 1950s.

Who are those cool young women walking through the airport smoking cigarettes with matching carry-on suitcases and flashy neck scarves?

Who is that diverse group of cool people wearing oversized wool scarves in August, eating soft pretzels together in the food court, and mocking people who try to refold jeans into the denim wall?

See? Same thing.

I began my tenure at the Gap over in the connected Gap Kids store area. I was handed a pocket sizing chart and left to deal with the moms who wandered in with their small ones looking for jeans and logo sweatshirts. I was originally excited to be over in Gap Kids because the clothes and tiny shoes were adorable, but quickly realized that working there was looked down upon the same way it was looked down upon to work at Gap Outlet. It was still the Gap, but not really.

Plus, I thought I'd be better with small children than I actually was. The kids in Gap Kids ads always looked so cool, and fun, and like they probably drank coffee and knew multiple languages because their parents pulled them out of school to take a gap year (get it?) traveling the world with only the wooden toys they could fit in their hemp knapsacks. In reality, the kids who shopped at the Gap were only there because their parents dragged them in, and they hated shopping as much as all the normal non-Gap kids, no matter how many stickers or panda-themed anorak jackets you threw at them.

If I had to put a number on it, I would say that 40 percent of all babies brought into the store were there because they accidentally pooped all over themselves and mom needed to buy a quick outfit to change them into. This was not the Gap prestige I had in mind.

I was eventually moved over into the main retail store, and I quickly learned the hierarchy of the floor positions. It went as follows:

GREETER. This sounds like a pretty friendly and easy task, but the early two thousands experienced the rise of the store credit card, so all greeters were armed with a clipboard and a personal goal to harass a minimum of five people into applying for a Gap credit card per shift. There are few things that will get you cussed out in the Gap, and this was one of them.

The Greeter was also largely responsible for loss prevention, but in the most ineffective way possible. We weren't allowed to actually do anything when people stole our clothes. We were told to follow them around the store, and try and make alternative clothing suggestions to them, perhaps offering them a complementary color alternative for the nine cardigans they'd clearly stuffed into their bags, but that was about it. Our theft-deterrent tool was guilt, and much like when my mom tries to shame me for not attending Mass regularly, like Sharon Gallagher's adult children do, and wonders whether she needs to get a cancerous mole removed from her back in order to get me to show up like Sharon does, it never worked.

GENERAL FLOAT. This employee's mission was to float about the store where needed, tidying up messy tables and displays, reminding people about the fucking credit cards, and directing them to the fitting room area.

FITTING ROOM ATTENDANT. I am Vinz Clortho, the Key Master. Obscure *Ghostbusters* reference aside, the fitting room attendant was the indentured servant of retail. While it was mighty powerful to move about the area with a ring of keys on your wrist, it also meant running all over to get new sizes for customers, and then reshelving all the clothes they decided not to buy, but left strewn about the dressing room floor. This position should be required training for anyone thinking of having kids. Lamaze and infant CPR, that's all very helpful, but a course in not burning your house down in rage after you pick up twenty pairs of inside-out jeans off the floor because they're not the right kind of blue is where the true lesson lies.

DENIM SPECIALIST. Some people go to school to be doctors, some people study for the bar exam, and some people attend an intensive weekend retreat in the back room of a mall to learn about washes, cuts, and the perfect jean fold.

Being assigned to the denim wall was reserved for only the most anal of retail employees, and they spent a great deal of time protecting it. When they weren't silently and meticulously folding and stacking denim by size and cut, they were racing in front of customers reaching for jeans in the hopes of preventing them from grabbing a pair from the bottom of a pile, holding them up in front of them, then rolling them back up and stuffing them into the shelf.

Employees on the verge of losing it were often sent to "the wall" to calm down; quietly folding and stacking the clean lines of jeans . . . it was like an enema for the soul.

Even now, I fold all my jeans and T-shirts to Gap specifications, much the way I imagine Subway sandwich artists who worked the line in the 1990s still scoop out the tops of their bread when making sandwiches. Speaking of, why did they ever stop doing this? Now all the meat just keeps falling out of the side.

REGISTERS. Now, this is where the cool kids were. All you had to do was stand there, take people's money, ask them if they wanted to add any Gap scents or lip glosses, and if you needed anything, you just pushed a button on your Britney Spears headset and called for the minions on the floor to do your bidding. If Henry VIII worked at the Gap, he'd be at the registers.

Everyone who worked on the floor largely despised the register employees, not only because they always had us running for things like price checks or new sizes, but when they experienced any downtime, instead of leaving their pedestals and helping tidy the store, they just leaned on the counter and chatted with the managers, acting all exhausted. As if printing out gift receipts was more mentally taxing than folding and organizing three hundred pairs of socks during a six-hour shift.

We plebes on the floor would all stare at them, thinking evil thoughts such as *There's fecal matter all over those twenties you're holding, Mackenzie.*

BACK ROOM. All the perks of the Gap discount, none of the stress of customers or sales goals. The people who worked in the back room opening boxes and sorting merchandise had it made. They could wear whatever they wanted, listen to songs not sung by Macy Gray, and they could eat the whole time. These spots were often reserved for veteran employees who'd grown jaded about the basic-tee life.

I was hired during Christmas my senior year of high school, and getting to drive thirty minutes from my village into the city of Toledo to hang out with a group of people who were diverse and fashionable and cool was a pretty big deal for someone who was not any of those things.

Brad was a music composition major home from college on holiday break, and the former long-term boyfriend of Nate, who was recently promoted to assistant manager. They rarely spoke directly to each other, but when Nate would go over floor assignments at the start of each shift, Brad would get his position for the day and then roll his eyes and stomp away dramatically the same way my brother did when my mom asked him to throw an empty bottle *in* the garbage can, not *next to* the garbage can.

Sometimes when Brad and I were stuck together folding and cleaning up a section after the store closed, he'd whisper that Nate was the type of gay man who hated himself for being gay. It was the kind of intimate conversation that hurt my chest and felt out of place next to a table full of knits.

"He'd never hold my hand in the mall," he said, thoughtlessly holding a T-shirt against his chest as he folded it. "Don't ever hate who you are. It makes you ugly."

Mimi was tall, thin, wore a uniform of all black, and had a sharp black bob that stopped directly at her chin. Her mouth was cut as sharply as her chin, and when she spoke to me, she was cold and always looked slightly past me, never in the eye.

One day she arrived for the evening shift beaming, her face flushed pink.

"Brittany, I've been dying to show you!" she screeched. "Look, I got engaged!"

She held her thin white hand in front of me, and I turned it to admire the large square diamond.

"Congratulations!" I told her, and she hugged me tightly before running off to show more people in the back room.

"Gosh." I leaned against the counter where Nate was writing out the morning sales numbers. "I always assumed she didn't like me."

"No, that's just her face." He sighed, not looking up.

The only other plus-size employee was Heather, a part-timer who worked as a teacher during the day and in the Gap Kids section most weeknights. She didn't really adhere to any sort of Gap aesthetic, choosing mostly black leggings under an oversized denim button-up shirt, but the kids loved her and she had the patience of Job, so she was a manager favorite.

In my small town, where people still sometimes wore Starter jackets to funerals, I was treated as unfashionable and ugly. I expected that feeling only to be magnified among this gang of cool kids, but they accepted me. They accepted me because I was funny, I let them talk about themselves, and it turns out that once you get out of high school, nobody really cares if their friends are fat, they only care that they're not assholes.

Working at the Gap was life changing.

I was placed in the fitting rooms, I suspect because I was terrible at counting out change and took "no" as an answer too quickly when it came to credit-card sign-up.

"Hi, would you like to sign up for a Gap credit card and save ten percent off your purchase today?"

"That card is a scam, get away from me, debt harpy."

"Okay, thanks, have a great day, don't forget all our flannel jammies are on sale this month!"

Working dressing rooms was like working on the front lines of a propaganda war. I helped people dress for Christmas parties, for wedding receptions, for funerals and first dates in clothes they wanted me to tell them they looked great in. And I did, even when they didn't.

I've looked them in the eye, smiled brightly, and said, "Hi, how many are you taking in today?" When what I really wanted to say was, "None of this will ever fit, don't let these jeans destroy you, save yourself."

"You are so much more than this beige linen dress."

"Deep breaths, there are only six people in the world who look good in corduroy overalls, and two of them are Olsen twins."

I imagine working in retail is similar to being a criminal lawyer when you know, for sure, your client is a murderer.

It was especially painful when I'd see a mother and plus-size daughter come in to shop. I had been that girl . . . hell, I still *was* her. I know what it's like to go into the store all the popular kids in your school are shopping at, and have to leave with a scarf.

I stood outside their fitting room door and heard the girl in tears because even if it did zip, and it did button, and it did go over her head, it didn't look right because it wasn't properly cut for anyone over a size 14. And I wish I could have recommended ten other places for these mothers and daughters to shop, but the truth is that I couldn't recommend even one. And of all the brands that were popular then—Abercrombie, Express, The Limited, and Guess—Gap had one of the most generous cuts out there. This was all long before Lane Bryant was in most malls, and even before the plus-size section of department stores had much besides floral grandma prints. You didn't even have the option to go online and buy cute leggings and jackets in your size that looked like what your friends were wearing and that you felt comfortable zipping. There were no options.

It was frustrating, especially for teen girls, not to be able to dress as trendy and youthful as their peers. But help was on the way, because in the fall of 2000, Gap released the men's boot-cut jean. Finally there was something somewhat equivalent to the popular flare jean everyone else my age was wearing.

Express flare jeans were peak 1999, and I could not fit into them. Undeterred, I had purchased the largest size they offered, washed them cold, and then worn them to bed soaking wet in the hope that by the time I woke up, they'd be stretched out and fit. They weren't and they didn't. When I woke they were still damp, smelled like mildew, and I was rocking a raging yeast infection.

But the Gap men's boot-cut jean gave me that lower-leg flare with a waist size that could accommodate my body. Granted, the crotch hung a little low on account of me not having a penis or testicles, but all of that was easily remedied by pulling the jeans up over my stomach, just below my bra. And thus, high-waist Brittany was born.

I began slowly introducing the men's jeans to the women in the dressing rooms; the ones I heard huffing and whimpering and weeping.

"Trust me," I whispered as I slid the jeans over the door.

Brad, our resident denim specialist, was horrified, and every time I'd jog out to the wall for armfuls of boot-cut jeans, he'd roll his eyes.

"These jeans are not cut for the womens, Brittany," he'd singsong to me.

"Very few are, Brad," I'd sing back as I walked away.

Soon, my curvy customers would send their friends and

daughters in to find me, and I'd unlock their doors with a knowing nod. We became a secret society, and I their leader, bestowing flared pants on those who had not previously had the option.

Yes, fat sisters, you are welcome here. Come. Graze. Try on your man pants and rejoice. Also, while you're here, may I interest you in a nice oversized men's logo sweatshirt or some Dream perfume?

When I went away to college, I transferred to a Gap down in Columbus, near my dorm at The Ohio State University, and eventually moved from the floor to the early-morning and overnight shift of people in charge of doing markdowns and rearranging the store. After four years in Gap servitude, I realized I was burned out on retail and customer service. Plus, in Gap years, four years is actually twenty-four years, and after twenty-four years, you just can't get excited about khaki pants anymore. But I had done a small service to my fellow woman.

This was my very first experience with body advocacy. Drawing attention to myself as a plus-size person who knew something about plus-size clothes was admitting to other people, in no uncertain terms, that I was fat. It was a big, important step.

While I might know I'm fat, have known I was fat, it was certainly not something I wanted the world to know out loud about me. I just assumed that when I talked with someone we both knew that when we spoke about gaining weight or being heavy, we weren't talking about me, we were talking about the other fat people. And yet there I was, standing in the witness protection area of a Gap fitting room waving my fat-girl flag.

Wearing those men's jeans was the first time my brain was willing to break up with the asinine idea that the only way to look beautiful lived and died on the tag of the pants I was trying to fit into.

A tag, might I add, that nobody could see but me.

CHAPTER 2

I Blame Cher Horowitz
For Everything

"Oof, Brittany, what happened to you, I can see your twinkle!"

Not quite the reveal I had expected. I was just returning to Swanton Junior High School after what my parents referred to as "my educational sabbatical."

I was not "transitioning well."

I was experiencing a "crisis of identity."

Everyone around me spoke in air quotes and soft voices and tilted their heads to the side in concern when they talked to and about me. Prior to my eighth-grade English teacher announcing to the class that she could see my vagina, I flew relatively under the radar in school. As a new kid the year before, I worked my way through the social ranks from loner to nerd, and was just settling into "stoner" when everything went pear-shaped.

The stoners were a relatively welcoming crew made up of kids across multiple cliques; some of them heavy-metal folk, some of them popular jocks, some of them random one-offs that didn't quite fit into any of the groups but could superficially participate because they were good at rolling joints or always had access to beer. I was a one-off. At least I was until I was dumped by my very first boyfriend (a stoner), and all of my friends began to shun me like the Amish. Like really stoned Amish, but instead of beards, they had that weird preteen lip hair. Naturally, since I was newer to the group than my boyfriend, he took ownership of our mutual friends. The girls I felt I had bonded with also chose to stay close to the group. They began ignoring my calls, glaring at me in the halls, and eventually three-way prank-calling me at home.

I don't think three-way calling is a thing anymore, but in the nineties it was a form of terrorism.

I became a girl without a lunch table. And eventually, when nobody wants to talk to you, you just stop talking. And that is what I did, for six months.

I didn't talk to kids at school, I didn't talk to my mom and dad, and I didn't talk to my brother. I came home every day, locked myself in my room, and watched VHS tapes. Naturally, this freaked my parents out, but they both worked long hours, so while they were confused that I wasn't speaking, they really didn't have the free time to properly look into it.

My mom would reach out to my ex-girlfriends looking for answers, unaware they didn't like me anymore. She sent a few notes to teachers and my guidance counselor, but everyone just assumed it was a weird side effect of teenage hormones. And then I stopped going to school.

Every morning my dad would try to drop me off at the door and I'd just melt down, sobbing and pleading for him to let me stay home just one more day. And he always did, mostly because putting up any sort of fight would have made him late for work.

To this day, I don't know the specifics of why I was allowed to remain home for almost two months, or what conversations there were between my parents and the school administrators. All I know is that my parents came home from work one day, told me I was finished going to school for a while, and walked out of my room. I didn't feel happy or a sense of victory about the announcement; I felt safe. And a week later, I started to talk again.

Movies are my love language. I grew up in the back room of my parents' video rental store, eating my dinner each night alongside Bill Murray, Steve Guttenberg, and Phoebe Cates. In fact, I've passed my cinema-obsessed vampire spirit onto my kids, and we spend their summer vacations in dark movie theaters with buttered popcorn and smuggled-in candy.

As expected, communication in my family was also often done through movies. When I won my first essay contest through our local library system, I came home to find the latest New Kids on the Block concert VHS tape on my bed as a reward. And when my parents saw that I was finally starting to speak to them again, my mom excitedly pushed a new movie into the VCR and snuggled onto the couch between me and my younger brother, Adam.

Clueless, a film starring the young Alicia Silverstone, was about a Beverly Hills High student who "selflessly" played matchmaker to her peers, advocated to save the environment, and eventually dated her stepbrother.

"This movie is ridiculous," Adam groaned, burying his face into a couch pillow in annoyance. "This is the stupidest movie you've ever made me watch."

This movie changed my life.

Cher Horowitz was everything I was not. She was rich, she had a beautiful house, the perfect body, and amazing clothes she pulled out of a robot closet.

I was decidedly not rich. In fact, at the time of that viewing, my family was getting our water out of a large metal tank in the backyard because our well point had died and we couldn't afford to replace it. So that ruled out the whole robot-walk-in-closet thing as well. But the preppy clothes and cute shoes were fantastic, and coming from Catholic school meant I had a whole closet full of ignored plaid skirts.

One of the hardest aspects of transferring into a new and bigger school was learning how to fit in and look like the other kids in my class, and girls had it especially tough. All the boys needed were baggy jeans and bowl cuts. For us girls, it was a delicate balance of showing up each day looking like the right kind of Bratz doll. The parameters were very specific. I had to try to look effortlessly hot, but not like a slut. I had to look like I was probably really good at blow jobs, but not like I'd given too many of them. I had to balance looking good enough for the boys to like me, but not so cute that the girls turned on me and hated me. This was a particularly delicate balance to achieve with big boobs, which, by default, had me carrying around a bit of a skanky scarlet letter. In short, *Mean Girls* wasn't a movie yet, but it *was,* so to speak, a documentary.

Nobody at my school was dressing like Cher Horowitz, and for some reason, I saw her as the key to my reentry into the general population. My debutante coming-out, if you will. Only instead of wearing white and making my entrance into southern society, I'd wear short skirts and hope no one carved KILL YOURSELF into my locker. I crafted a four-step plan.

First, I had to talk my parents into letting me trade in my gold-wired glasses for contacts. This was a tough sell to my mother, who had a lifelong belief that everyone was just one human touch away from sepsis. She'd shove my brother and me outside from morning until night during the summer to entertain ourselves doing God knows what, but the second I tried to walk into a petting zoo, she had me scrubbing up to my elbows like Meredith Grey.

"Do you know how much fecal matter is on the human finger?" she whisper-yelled to me in the dark exam room of my ophthalmologist's office when he left the room to grab my contact samples.

Next, I asked my dentist to fill the gap between my two front teeth with bonding. I want to break in here and say, if I could take anything in my life back, it would be this act. More on it later.

Third, one of my hair-stylist aunts scooped up my coarse, frizzy hair and gave me my first real hairstyle that wasn't just a vague geometric shape like "triangle."

And lastly, I had my mom cut off and hem all my plaid Catholic school skirts.

"Shorter." I stood beside her sewing machine.

For as little interest as I've watched my mother take in fashion and beauty, she never told me no. The issues that I have with my body and feeling bad about it never came from her. She always treated hers with such indifference. She wore what was comfortable, she shopped in whatever section she felt like, and she was never on a diet. My insecurities came from other people telling me I should have them.

The decision to return to school was a hard one, and my parents briefly toyed with the idea of transferring me to a school in a different district altogether, but in the end decided that sending me back to face my fears was the best course of action. At the time, I did not agree with this decision, but here I am writing a book about it, so thanks for the emotional material, Mom and Dad.

I walked into my eighth-grade English class with my silky flat-ironed "Rachel" haircut, and a plaid skirt hemmed so short that when I sat down my esophagus touched the seat of the chair. I paired it with a white cropped baby tee, and white thigh-highs that I'd purchased from the pharmacy out of one of those panty-hose eggs. On Cher, white thigh-highs looked adorable and adolescent. On my thick dimpled thighs, they looked pornographic, or at least they would have if they hadn't rolled down to my ankles like some kind of doughnut with every step.

I walked into English and immediately made eye contact with Mike Miller, a senior boy who helped grade papers in the class for extra credit. Mike had long hair, quoted *Romeo and Juliet,* and always looked duly troubled and charmingly angsty. He had been my favorite part of English class, and in a completely nonstalker move, I'd figured out that he worked as a delivery boy for a local pizza shop. I'd made my mom order pizza every Friday she was paid, hoping to see him at our door.

As I made my way to a desk in the back, I bent over to re-roll the white nylons up my legs, and just then, the teacher walked in behind me.

"Oof, Brittany, what happened to you, I can see your twinkle!" she declared, resting her right hand against her chest.

To save face, I'd like to interject right here that the Friday after this happened, Pizza Mike asked me out. He wrote his number on the box of the thick-crust pineapple-and-green-pepper pizza he delivered; total rom-com move. The date, however, wasn't. This was because he brought along his friend Lance and they spent the whole night getting high, listening to Bob Marley, and watching old episodes of *Felix the Cat* with the sound off.

But before I knew all of that, having my "twinkle" called out by my teacher was absolutely humiliating. Today that teacher probably would have been fired after my mom created a viral social media post about her singling out my vagina for comment. But it was the nineties and parents weren't super indignant about the coddling of their kids yet. So I excused myself from class early and called my parents from the office to pick me up. The secretary was very understanding, nodding softly and clucking with her tongue that I might just have to "ease my way back in."

Have you ever been so determined to fit in with people that you show up at school dressed as the adult-fetish-film version of a popular teen icon? My chubby Cher Horowitz phase was short-lived, but it became the first of many times I tried to become someone else in an attempt to avoid just being me.

A professor in college once told me that if you wanted to know about a woman's love history, look in her closet. It's overflowing with the ghosts of relationships past hung on hangers and sorted by season. This analogy can best describe my life in high school: desperate and unoriginal.

The bedroom closet at my parents' house is the only part of my old room they maintained after I moved out, turning the rest into what my mom affectionately calls her "pug room," which is just a room with a couch and television where she sits with all her pugs and watches HGTV. Yes, I would have liked to one day have it serve as a museum of my childhood, but in a fifteen-hundred-square-foot ranch, that kind of empty space is prime real estate for dog-show trophies and flea-market paintings of pugs playing poker and smoking cigars.

In the wall-length closet, hidden behind the dust-and-dog-hair-covered louver doors, you'll find all the clothes from all the styles and hobbies I'd picked up and dropped based on the boys I dated, or wish I could have dated, in high school.

I know what this looks like. Brittany: Single White Female. But I was totally harmless and my therapist tells me all the time that it's totally normal for teenage girls to chameleon around a bit as they figure out who they are. Also, I don't have the face shape for a Bridget Fonda pixie cut, I just don't.

There was the skater, Elton. He and his friends spent every free moment skateboarding at the underused parking lot of a local grocery store. Prior to "talking" to him, which is this thing teens do when one of you totally wants to date, but the other one is afraid to tell you no, I dressed the way many insecure chubby junior high girls dressed in the nineties: part *Blossom,* part Avril Lavigne, part *The Craft,* because a flannel around the waist hides everything. Hanging out with Elton presented a new set of style influences, all of them cringe-worthy and mostly unwashed.

Elton had chin-length brown hair and wore saggy jeans and old skater tennis shoes. Each day that I sat watching him grind and alley-oop, my clothing and vocabulary evolved, until eventually I was beside him, flipping off the police who demanded we leave the private property, with my obnoxious JNCO wide-leg jeans, white tank top, and brightly colored bra. It was as if I was aiming for skater, but got lost somewhere between No Doubt and Seth Green in *Can't Hardly Wait*. I carried a skateboard catalog in my back pocket for weeks, always under the guise of trying to decide on a board and finally learning to skate.

Thankfully, Elton started dating someone else before I did something really ridiculous, like buy Airwalks or break my neck. But still, the jeans hang untouched in my old closet.

Vince was also a metal head, and he and his buddies were known throughout school as the Black T-shirt Gang. Every day it was black heavy-metal T-shirts and black jeans. If you were ever curious as to why men's black classic-cut jeans existed, I can assure you, it was because of Vince and his crew.

Dating Vince for six months came with a whole host of wardrobe accommodations. It started off small with black jeans and a couple of mildly violent Slayer shirts, and eventually steamrolled into the single most expensive piece of clothing I'd ever owned, a genuine black leather jacket from a store in the mall called Leather Unlimited.

This jacket was a big deal. Think Pink Ladies–level membership; only, you know, not pink or formfitting or flattering in any way. When I initially asked my mom to buy me this jacket, because I was in seventh grade and had no disposable leather jacket income, she laughed in my face and went back to shaving the hair off the back of the cocker spaniel she'd been grooming for our neighbor. It took weeks of coaxing and begging, eventually striking the deal that I could get the jacket as my one and only Christmas gift. In hindsight, a girl should never sacrifice all her Christmas gifts for a black leather stoner jacket, but Vince was my first French kiss and we'd planned to get matching Grim Reaper tattoos when we were eighteen, so naturally, it felt worth it at the time.

I got the jacket in December and Vince dumped me on my birthday in April. The jacket hadn't even been broken in yet. It was still stiff, creaked when I walked, and smelled like a new car. While it pained me to think of how much money my parents had scraped together to buy me that jacket, I was instantly relieved not to have to wear it and pretend to understand Pantera lyrics anymore.

And then there was Josh the pagan. I come from a hyper-Catholic family. I attended Catholic school, we went to church on Sundays, we didn't eat meat during Lent, and I could assemble a rosary in my sleep. My middle name is Marie, which means Mary, and you don't get more Catholic than the mother of Christ.

Naturally, I was ready to throw that all out the window when I met Josh, or as my grandmother liked to call him, the heathen kid from public school. Josh wore layers of hemp and puka-shell necklaces, always smelled like incense, and smoked clove cigarettes. He was also a member of a coven of witches, and did not go to my school, which automatically made him the coolest, most mysterious person I knew.

Interfaith relationships can sometimes be tricky, but watching Josh worship at a tiny altar in his basement bedroom was kind of a turn-on. It also could have been all the pot we smoked. Josh never so much asked me to change my style, but I started to feel uncomfortable around him dressing as I normally did. Once he took me to a bonfire to meet his friends, and everything I was wearing began to feel destructive to the environment. Pink furry mohair sweaters are about as biodegradable as a plastic bottle.

Because I came from a lower-middle-class family, and my parents had already blown their wads on a barely worn leather jacket, altering my look for this relationship was a bit of an arts-and-crafts project. First, I gathered all the white clothing I had, mostly tank tops and the dress I wore for my eighth-grade confirmation, and spent an entire week tie-dyeing it. It was like a Phish concert had taken place in my bedroom.

Step two in the "Brittany Renounces the Son of God and Dabbles in Paganism for a Boy" process had me buying a pentacle necklace from Spencer's Gifts. It was a BOGO situation, so I also grabbed a patchouli candle and a Coexist bumper sticker for my dad's station wagon.

And the final—albeit worst—step in this transformation took place on my head. Two words: faux dreadlocks. Like Jennifer Aniston at the Emmys, I twisted my hair into phony dreadlocks with sticky gel and stuck a daisy barrette or two in there for good measure.

Now, as I look at the rainbow-dyed dresses in my closet and stray hemp chokers in the jewelry box on the shelf, I am reminded why our love faltered. Pagan Josh and Harry Potter were not the same thing. Josh wanted to walk in the woods and listen to nature for hours and hours. Harry Potter went to an awesome wizard school, had wands, and used magic to defend himself. Josh's and my concept of magic was not the same as Harry's. Plus, Josh started to get really irritated when I asked him to cast spells for things like unlimited bowls of pasta. I should have just dated the Olive Garden; at least then I wouldn't have had to stop shaving under my arms.

Now, you might have gotten to the end of this list and thought, *Wow, that is an excessive amount of pandering to keep a boyfriend, Brittany.* Like Julia Roberts in *Runaway Bride*, the movie in which she always orders her eggs in the identical manner as the man to whom she is currently engaged . . . with Brian it is scrambled, Gill is fried, George likes them poached, and with Coach Bob she is an egg-whites-only girl. The eggs are a giant metaphor for finding out who she really is by stepping back and figuring out how she likes her eggs all on her own.

The difference between me and Julia Roberts was that she didn't know who she was, hence, a two-hour movie plot. I actually knew *exactly* who I was; it's just that I assumed nobody would want me. I became an "I'll have what he's having" type of girl because I assumed that what I could create would be a more palatable option. The wide-leg jeans and puka-shell chokers and the leather jacket were all calculated changes to make my appearance more "acceptable."

None of it actually worked, of course. I had spent a huge amount of time morphing into identical versions of the boys I'd chased after, when none of them ended up with clones of themselves, anyways. Elton married a popular girl from choir. Josh is still dating around, and according to Facebook, no longer Wiccan. And after Vince dumped me on my birthday, he went on to date all sorts of girlie girls who never once had to buy their own leather jacket to impress him.

I had to wait for the boy who liked me for who I actually was, and not some crazy extended version of the guy I was trying to copy. Which is a good thing, because the next boy I fell in love with thought he was a white rapper, and I simply don't have the neck strength for gold chains.

CHAPTER 3

The Word You're Looking For Is "Fat"

All right, it's early, so let's just get it out of the way. Before I was all about confidence and body love, there was a time when the worst thing you could call me was fat. I remember coming home from parties in high school and having my mom apply Icy Hot to my neck, shoulders, and back after I'd spent a night tense and fearful that someone would whisper something about my weight. I was petrified of being laughed at behind my fellow students' red cups of cheap beer.

It's ironic, then, that being called fat as an adult is exactly what turned me into the openly plus-size woman I am today. There I was online, blogging about being a mom and a wife, being funny and witty and really cool. I had tens of thousands of readers a month who followed my posts and liked my social media updates. I was the popular girl for the first time ever, because, guys, it's shockingly easy to create an awesome fake life on the Internet. I mean, obviously, look at the show *Catfish*.

Unlike *Catfish*, I wasn't really trying to be a totally different person, and all the words and thoughts I shared were true, but the photos I put up of myself were not. They were always heavily edited or artistically cropped in ways that helped me appear a lot thinner than I actually was.

And then one day someone from my hometown found a photo of me from a friend's baby shower on Facebook and tagged me in the picture, publicly called me out, and told everyone that I altered my photos to hide the fact that I was really just a fat woman pretending to be thin. Which was actually a completely, albeit shitty, true thing to say, because that is exactly what I was doing. It was humiliating and I thought that it would be the end of my social media career.

As it turns out, people didn't care that I wasn't skinny, and they didn't stop reading my blog. Instead, I was bombarded by women saying "me too!," "you're just like me!," "I love you even more."

And suddenly, being called fat wasn't a death. I'd lived, and—dare I say—thrived, since it happened in the most public and embarrassing way.

Did I love being called fat? No, but I also think it's silly to define people by what they look like. I don't call my friend Eric "One Shorter Leg Eric," or my UPS guy Brian "White

Stuff in the Corner of His Mouth Brian." I just call them Eric and Brian, and everyone else does, too. Okay, actually we call Eric "Free Ride Eric," but that's because he always forgets his wallet.

A few years ago, after my public "outing," I sat down with the marketing department of a large clothing brand to discuss the copy used in the plus-size editions of their fall catalogs. I was seated at a long wooden table, surrounded by four men with notebooks in front of them, and past catalogs spread out before me. You know, exactly how you would assume meetings about what women like to call themselves would go.

The men's concern was that the use of the term "plus size" insulted consumers and made them feel unattractive.

I explained that I didn't find "plus size" to be a pejorative term, it was simply a practical way to organize clothing sizes. When breaking down a catalog of clothing, petite, tall, and plus size are all very normal descriptors. What was making women feel unattractive was what the clothing companies were making "plus size" mean.

What clothing companies needed to understand was that women don't fall into two categories—women and plus-size women. We're all just women. And that reality should be reflected in how we're being marketed to and designed for as consumers.

I asked the marketing team what the average age of their straight-size customer was, and the answer was twenty-eight years old.

"And what about the plus-size demographic?" I asked.

"It's the same," they answered.

It's the same, and yet every plus-size look in that catalog back then skewed older and more modest than the straight sizes, both in styling and fit. Photos of thin models in deep V-neck dresses was in contrast to the plus-size version of the same dress, which was either cut much higher or modified with a tacky scarf around the neck. The problem wasn't that they were calling us plus size. The problem was that they thought plus-size women wanted to hide their bodies, and buy ugly prints and unflattering cuts. Don't get me started on the excess of glitter, sequins, and shimmer to be found on plus-size clothes. This is supposed to be workwear, guys. We aren't clowns. We aren't living our lives at a perpetual Ugly Christmas Sweater party.

I flipped open the two catalogs, and compared the photos of the curvy beautiful women with the straight-size catalog. The plus-size models were photographed alone, as if they were always caught contemplating some sort of solo *Eat, Pray, Love* journey. They were all staring wistfully out the window of a plain room, as if they were just waiting for their lives to begin.

Women in the straight-size catalog were always photographed alongside men, and sometimes also children. They were smiling, laughing, carrying flowers, riding bikes, having a social life, and doing normal things like being in love or raising children.

Being fat can already feel isolating. By removing the possibility or suggestion of love, companionship, or family in those plus-size photos, this marketing strategy drove the point home in a painful, subliminal way.

We get it. We're fat and going to die alone in modestly cut knit dresses that hit lower on the leg than the ones the skinny girls are wearing.

I don't care what you call my clothes. Plus-size jeans, fat-girl jeans . . . heck, you could call them herpes pants, and I'd still buy them as long as they fit well and look like something a thirty-six-year-old woman who likes to tell people she is twenty-eight, gets laid on the regular, has sexy underwear, and likes a bottle of wine sometimes wants to wear.

Plus-size women want to wear the same exact clothes as thin women, in the same exact way. It's just that many of us are still trying to figure out how to do that. Luckily, I had a few teachers.

I've always been one of those people who watch movies, and get so lost inside them that I inhabit them long after I've stood up and walked out of the theater. Not even walking outside into a blinding sun jolts me back into reality.

I spend whole days as Sally from *Practical Magic* or Bella Swan from *Twilight*.

My Anastasia Steele phases are legendary.

This very modest form of cosplay is how I taught myself how to figure out fashion. I didn't really know who I was, or how to put anything together for long stretches of my life, so I took characters that I saw on-screen and copied their style, modifying it to what I could find in my size.

It's similar to how my dad taught himself how to remove staples from his own scalp by watching YouTube videos.

It's a process that I still totally fuck up sometimes. This is why my Facebook page is set to require my approval for all tags. Yes, this is partially so I'm not tagged in the background of photos where I'm shoveling nachos into my gaping maw, but also because even I don't want to relive my Zooey Deschanel bangs unless I give consent.

The very first house my husband and I ever bought did not have closets. Technically, I am not even sure you can call a room without closets a bedroom, but we called it that and we had three such rooms. We were just so excited to be able to purchase a home, we really didn't care that we had no place to store our belongings.

Thankfully, I spent the majority of our time in that house either pregnant or caring for infants, so the limited wardrobe I'd had was either being worn, washed, on the floor covered in poop, or in a basket. If digging through a basket of clean clothes was an Olympic sport, I'd be doped up and holding a gold medal right now.

We've since moved into a bigger home, but had the chance to go back and walk through our previous residence when it went up for sale. It was like going on a mission trip to Calcutta. Clothes were hung on nails on the wall and slung over furniture, clutter was everywhere, and I needed

to dry-swallow a Xanax to make it through our old bedroom.

But it reminded me how far we'd come. How far *I'd*
come.

The house didn't look like an overflowing storage unit
when I lived there because I really didn't have enough
clothes to make a mess with. Some leggings, a couple of
stretched-out nursing bras, oversized T-shirts I stole from
my dad, and a pair of maternity jeans. Now I have my
own closet, and have taken over another room in our
house, not because I'm Mariah Carey, but because I'm excited about fashion, I like taking care of the pieces I save
for and buy, and honestly, cluttered rooms give me panic
attacks.

I'm not here to be buried in a coffin filled with rompers.
And I'm excited about fashion because in the years since I
began working on fashion campaigns, I've noticed something. A change. Companies have finally woken up and
taken note of the curvy girl. Plus-size fashion is the single
biggest growth area in retail right now. This is incredibly
exciting. Take a look online and embrace our new reality.
I'm not just talking about Target and Old Navy. I'm talking
about amazing brands for every budget. I'm talking about
all the major department stores out there with extensive
plus-size collections. I'm talking about major marquee-
name supermodels who are size 14 and above landing on
the cover of *Glamour* and *Vogue,* and not just for the plus-
size edition. Michael Kors, Calvin Klein, Junarose, Univer-

sal Standard, Vince Camuto, Lucky, ASOS, Eloquii, and so many more brands offer amazingly cute, fashion-forward clothes for us. And not a damn sparkle in sight.

That's not to say that we don't still get short-shrifted in some ways. We can't go and try this stuff on 90 percent of the time. And plus-size clothes do tend to be pricier. But I look at it this way—if variety is the spice of life, then my life feels a hell of a lot spicier now than it did when I was a teenager and trying to cram myself into the biggest size I could find at Sears.

Last year I came across an Internet meme that used one of my bikini photos, and it said "Any Thick Girls Awake?" across the front in a white font.

A few weeks later, that same photo was also stolen by a dating site touting the headline: CHEATING PLUS SIZE WIVES SEEKING MEN OVER 30 FOR AFFAIRS.

I think we can all agree that last one is ridiculous. Seeking men over thirty? I already have one of those. So not only did they steal my copyrighted photo, they created a completely inaccurate portrayal of why I'd need a man over thirty, which is definitely not for affairs.

How about CHEATING PLUS-SIZE WIVES SEEKING MEN OVER 30 . . . for meaningful conversation about the underlying plot lines of *Gilmore Girls*.

CHEATING PLUS-SIZE WIVES SEEKING MEN OVER 30 . . . to help fill out the online rebate code thing for the new flat-screen. My husband asked me to do it months ago, but I forgot, and it might be too late, so hurry.

CHEATING PLUS-SIZE WIVES SEEKING MEN OVER 30 . . . to take all the expired food out of the fridge because it makes me want to puke. Just throw the whole Tupperware thing away, I don't even care.

CHEATING PLUS-SIZE WIVES SEEKING MEN OVER 30 . . . to ask my dad to stop calling me on speakerphone when he's in the bathroom.

CHEATING PLUS-SIZE WIVES SEEKING MEN OVER 30 . . . to condense the entire six seasons of *Game of Thrones* into one sentence that I can use at parties and work-related get-togethers. I actually don't watch this series, but hate being left out of pop-culture vernacular.

The point is they were using my photo and size to lure in men, which is *gross* because I'm not a fetish and *illegal* because I own the photo.

But what was interesting about this whole thing was that I wasn't upset that they called me plus size, and I wasn't upset that they called me thick. Back to that whole new-found-confidence thing. And "thick"? That one is especially appealing.

When I look in the mirror and see my thighs rubbing together and my boobs spilling out of my bra, I think, *Yes, I am what the Commodores were singing about. I am a Brick House.* I am sexy and solid and mighty; words I never thought could coexist.

When my kids crash into me, wrapping their arms around my legs, I know I am sound and rooted in the ground.

When Andy grabs the back of my waist in bed, I am as soft and voluptuous as I am substantial and present.

I have friends who hate being referred to as thick. They take it to only mean fat, which they find offensive. I am ecstatic to have powerful and provocative words like "thick" and "plus" describe my body. Instead of being sexy despite being heavy, I'm just sexy.

"Any thick girls awake?"

I am.

CHAPTER 4

We Called Her the Beast

We called her the Beast.

A name usually reserved for X-Men or intimidating dogs, but she was none of those. The Beast was a white lace, racer-back bra with padded foam cups that my friend Jordan and I stole from a garage sale our freshman year of high school.

I don't know what kind of person sells underwear at garage sales, and as an adult, I hold the people who buy their underwear at such venues in even lower esteem. But when you're a teenager and all your bras look like they come from the prop department of *The Sound of Music*, you get desperate.

I met Jordan when my mom signed me up for our local rec summer softball league in junior high, and she and I bonded on the bench complaining about how hot and miserable we were, and that the coach only looked at our chests when he gave us the batting order.

She was actually really popular, and I'd normally say something like, "I have no idea why she was hanging out with me," but the reality is that I knew exactly why we became friends. Jordan was the friend that understood me.

We were both chubby in high school; the difference was that Jordan was the better kind of chubby. She was the curvy kind, with dark Italian skin, bouncy boobs, a round butt, and brown curly hair. She had the kind of body any adult male would go crazy over, but that the moronic and shallow boys in high school labeled as fat.

In contrast, my body was more a long, droopy kind of chubby. Like you built a body out of Silly Putty, but then left it on the dash of your car on a hot day for like an hour. All of my skin drooped down, even my boobs.

Jordan was the only friend I had with whom I could share clothes and talk about my body, and that made us virtually inseparable throughout high school.

The story of the Beast begins in the garage of Brent, a senior boy who lived across the street from me. Despite being largely a flop with boys in my own grade, I spent a lot of time with the senior guys, and I brought Jordan along for all of the fun.

It was a literal girl-next-door situation, as in, I lived next door and they felt sorry for me, so they invited me over to hang out and drink their parents' beer. And eventually, yeah, hormones made things weird, as they do. I think that's pretty normal, it's why little kids play doctor, right? You can't have a room full of teenage genitals lying around and just expect people not to do anything with them.

The first time we played strip poker, I was terrified. There were five of us, and Jordan and I were the only girls. Naturally, I did not know how to play poker, which is how all good pornos start, but I escaped relatively unscathed, having just come from soccer practice, which allowed me to insist that I count each shin guard as an individual piece of clothing.

The next time did not work out as well. First losing my shirt, leaving me exposed in a bra with all the sexual appeal of Matlock. And then finally, with yet another terrible hand, the bra had to go as well.

The boys around me leaned closer into the table, eyebrows raised and lips wet. I struggled with the nine hooks along the back closure, making panicked eye contact with Jordan, who was also confined to her seat, underwearless and giggling.

I exhaled forcefully and, in one quick move, ripped the bra from my chest and tossed it with a thud on the table in front of us.

The boys looked from my face to my chest to my face again, confused.

"Where are your boobs?" Brent asked, baffled.

"They're here." I looked down at my lap. "Below, um. Below the table."

"Your boobs are so big they hang below the table!" One of the guys laughed.

"So do yours," Jordan shot back at them, always having my back and gathering our clothes to leave.

"Hey, we're sorry." They pleaded, standing and covering themselves with shirts and socks as we made our way to the door. Insecure me would have turned around and stayed, but Jordan wasn't having it.

We made our way back to my house barefoot through the wet grass, pulling our clothes back onto our bodies, both of us quiet and replaying the events of the night in our heads.

"We need better bras," I finally whispered as we crawled back through my bedroom window.

"We need to learn how to play poker," Jordan answered.

Hanging out with the boys next door became a form of workshopping. The same way a composer and lyricist try out new productions in front of small audiences to work out the quirks and refine musical numbers, we used the guys to privately figure out how to attract and date people without any of the social consequences brought on by dealing with actual boys in our grade.

We were like Lin-Manuel Miranda, only instead of writing *Hamilton,* we were workshopping things like blow jobs, French kissing, and how to talk to boys. My teen years were an R-rated John Hughes movie.

To this day, I cannot tell you what size the Beast was, only that when we brought it home and put it on, it fit both

Jordan and me perfectly. This was straight *Sisterhood of the Traveling Pants*–level shit, you guys. And it made our boobs look like magic. From the front. It made our boobs look like magic *from the front;* from the sides and back it was all back fat and spillover. But we were teenagers; fashion wasn't three-dimensional for us yet. I wore a dress that didn't zip to an honors ceremony the year before and just walked backward the whole time assuming people wouldn't notice.

The Beast was the bra I had to pack in my bag in order to leave the house, and change into once I was away from my parents. The racer back and cup padding raised my cleavage so high up my chest that I had to push it back down in order to chew. Jordan and I passed the bra between us every weekend, through making out with Mike or getting to third base with Beau. We'd play paper, rock, scissors before games of strip poker, the loser sweeping the table fully clothed and the winner batting her eyes like a Victoria's Secret Angel.

Our Spanish class took a trip to Mexico my junior year of high school, and Jordan and I packed the Beast in our luggage. We traded off evenings in her dancing to Will Smith songs in sweaty all-night discos, before peeling La Bestia from our damp skin, washing her in the sink, and hanging her to dry while we slept three hours before having to wake, board a non-air-conditioned bus hungover, and try not to vomit as we circled the ruins of Tulum and Chichén Itzá.

I want to add that this trip was severely underchaperoned, and we were left completely unsupervised every evening, free to wander around a foreign country, collect stamps on our hands from bars, and spend all night at dance clubs drinking giant tubes of frozen liquor. I have no idea what my parents were thinking.

During a particularly frantic white-girl dance break to "Barbie Girl" by Aqua in a *discoteca* in a Mérida, Mexico, the Beast sustained what would prove to be a mortal wound. The right underwire snapped, and despite our best efforts to remedy the situation with electrical tape and the travel sewing kit my mom swore I'd need for the trip, we could not save her.

Jordan and I limped (totally intoxicated because, remember, we were minors alone in Mexico) to the ocean, holding our heels in one hand, and half of the Beast in the other. We found a piece of cardboard, and using Jordan's lighter, lit the corner on fire, placed the Beast on top, and sent it afloat into the ocean.

"*I'm a Barbie girl, in a Barbie wooorld . . .*" we slurred softly, standing on the beach hand in hand. "*Life in plastic.*" I hiccuped. "*It's fantastic.*"

The Beast would get her Viking funeral.

BRAS. YOU'RE DOING IT WRONG.

Age does not bring forth knowledge when it comes to bras. Nor does it bring better boobs to put inside of them.

I swear, if I played strip poker right now, I could be sitting on a barstool, laying my cards down on a coffee table, and my nipples would still hang below the table. This is just the hand I've been dealt; I have large, heavy breasts.

At eight years old, I tried to bind them down with ACE bandages; at seventeen, I stuffed them into any push-up bras I could get my hands on; and then somewhere around age twenty-five, they began to rest comfortably in my armpits every time I lay down.

When it comes to boobs, we always want what we can't have. I see women with smaller chests and am envious of the thought of going braless or wearing a halter top without fighting a strapless bra. I'd love to make it through a summer without having to put deodorant around my chest or powder over the rashes I get from the heat and sweat.

I have a friend who constantly laments that her nipples get hard while she's working in her cold office, and I think, *Yeah, that never happens to me because my nipples point down and are sometimes wrapped around the underwire of my bra.*

I went to a fraternity party in college once with a Skittle taped to the inside center of each cup, trying to look like I had hard nipples. It totally worked the first hour, until I got too sweaty from dancing, the tape got damp, and the Skittles started to migrate all over the place. It was like my boobs were googly eyes. What I wouldn't give to walk around in a shirt too thin to hide actual hard round nipples looking youthful and sexual and womanly.

It's funny what we pick up on out of envy, right? Sometimes we stuff our bras, sometimes we make fake nipples out of candy . . . listen, boob insecurity can make you crazy.

As someone who's been in a bra for twenty-eight years, I feel I have enough seniority and experience to confidently tell you that all this is normal; bras are terrible, and everything you know about them is wrong.

There was a period of time, not long ago, when my bras tried to kill me. I'd be doing an everyday task, and mid-movement, *snap!*

You know those medical-miracle news stories where they show X-rays of dudes with nails in their heads that somehow missed every vital area? One day you will see my chest cavity on the screen with a U-shaped wire narrowly missing my beating heart. That or one of those "oh crap, what's in my rectum" X-rays. Andy and I are into butt stuff, it could go either way.

But in terms of boobs, while a bra is the most important thing I can put on to support them, doing so has meant that for the first three decades of my life, I have been in a seriously abusive relationship with my breasts.

I want to be really poetic here and say, "Oh, but they are beautiful vessels that nourished my children," but the truth is, they suck. They are bulky, they make my neck and back hurt, and even though it takes no less than a decade to grow out a set of bangs, the single hair on my right boob can go from root to rattail in a twelve-hour span. I have a lot of reasons to dislike my boobs. But it turns out, I just didn't understand how to take care of them.

THE CARE AND KEEPING OF YOUR BOOBIES

Like I said in the beginning of this book, I don't want this to be some sort of snore-fest how-to manual, but some things are really important, and measuring for a bra properly is one of them. Plus, we're friends now, and this is what friends do. We share clothes, hold each other's hair in the bar bathroom, and pinkie-swear to always make sure each other's boobs look amazing.

Why is it important to wear the correct-size bra? Well, for starters, you're going to look thinner. Wearing the correct-size bra added three inches to my torso, which had previously been covered by sagging boobs. By default, your clothes will also look better, and you'll stand up straighter because all of the weight you were previously dragging around with your shoulders will now be perfectly balanced in your cups and band.

I have been professionally measured twice, and both times I left with a bag full of expensive 36 DDDs. Yet I was still spilling over the tops of the cups of my bras, wire snaps, sore, red indents in my shoulders, and side boob fat.

Is this where I line up for the bra burning? Because these things suck.

It turns out, after watching numerous YouTube videos, which is how my generation learns to do things like lay tile flooring, make sushi, or squirt, I was being measured for a bra in the completely wrong manner. Which, looking back, makes sense. Every time I was measured by someone, they did so while I was wearing a bra. How on earth can you tell what size my boobs are by wrapping a tape measure around the crappy bra I already owned and walked in wearing?

Properly measuring yourself for a bra is something you can do completely by yourself in the privacy of your own house, and that can be done in three easy steps.

Now take your bra off and lock the door, because yeah, you can do this in your house, but it's not a sexy thing for anyone to walk into, the same way I'll never let Andy catch me shaving my toes.

You'll need a fabric-measuring tape, a pencil, and a piece of paper.

1. Take the measuring tape, wrap it around your rib cage where your bra band would sit, and exhale. Write down that number, it's your band size. *Mine is 38.*

2. Bend over at a ninety-degree angle. Yup, your boobs should be dangling and it's suddenly coming back to you why you always wear a bra during doggy style. Wrap the measuring tape loosely around your back and dangling bust, and write that number down. *Mine is 49.*

3. Now it's time for some math. Take those two numbers and subtract them (i.e., 49 − 38 = 11). Now take that number and check out the chart below to determine your cup size. *Tip: Most online*

*ordering is done in UK sizing, which is way more ac-
curate than U.S. sizing, govna!*

Differences in Inches:	US Cup Size	UK Cup Size
1″	A	A
2″	B	B
3″	C	C
4″	D	D
5″	DD or E	DD
6″	F	E
7″	G	F
8″	H	FF
9″	I	G
10″	J	GG
11″	K	H
12″	L	HH
13″	M	J
14″	N	JJ
15″	O	K

I am a 38H. AAAAAAAAAAA-CH. I'll admit that when
I first measured myself correctly, I went through various
stages of grief, such as throwing the measuring tape across
the room and calling it a liar, crying, texting my friend Meredith and telling her everything on the Internet was stupid,
putting my head between my knees and breathing slowly,
and then eventually accepting the truth.

Then I did the next naturally rational thing and

googled what the average cup size of a porn star was. It turns out, the answer to that question was a B, which didn't quite match the *Debbie Does Dallas* stereotype in my head.

That B cup makes my H cups sound downright cartoonish. Seriously, who would be into these things besides the cast of *Porky's*?

As a kid, I spent a lot of time sleeping over at friends' houses while my parents worked, and as a result, I became like "one of the family" to a few different sets of pals. One in particular, Olivia, lived with her grandmother Dot, a tiny old woman who stood about as high as my collarbone and had gigantic boobs. She was easily 70 percent breasts, and was always spilling food on her chest and complaining that her back hurt. I remember going to the bathroom and seeing her giant shiny nude bras hang-drying across the shower rod.

When I think of 38H boobs, I think of Dot.

This idea that society has put in our heads that the perfect woman has a big ass, tiny waist, and DDs is not an accurate one, for many, many reasons. But the main one is that the pictures of the women we see that are built like that don't actually have double-D breasts. Their breasts are much, much larger. But admitting you are a 42F doesn't sound as sexy as saying you've got double Ds. Hence the apprehension about being properly measured.

UGH, JUST TRY IT. I hear it almost every time.

"Um, yeah, I am not a [insert larger size here]."

Actually, you probably are. The measuring system we've all been subject to isn't accurate; it's just, you know, *available*. I was being fit into what was *available* to me in stores based on what society thinks is an appropriate size to offer, and I accepted it because I was terrified of being abnormal or large or different . . . when the fact is, I'm not any of those things. And neither are *you*.

IT MIGHT TAKE YOU A MINUTE. As a woman, I've experienced virtually zero standard of sizing across any other form of fashion. I can purchase the same-size jeans from three different stores, but depending on each brand's personal fit, sizing chart, and the country the jeans were produced in, none of them will fit the same. The same thing applies to bras. You might have to try a few different brands to find the one that best fits your assets.

SCOOP AND SWOOP. You know that stuff that oozes out of the sides of your bra? That's not armpit fat (okay, maybe it's a little armpit fat), that is actual boob. And it turns out, it's supposed to be scooped up and sit in the cup of the bra. All you have to do is slightly lean forward, and scoop all the breast tissue out from under your armpit, and push it forward.

If you try my bra-measuring method and find the bra is too big, it may be because you haven't swooped and scooped yet. Try it before you e-mail me to tell me I'm an idiot.

BUT EVERYTHING IS UGLY. Yeah, for a while there, larger bra options were total dogs. But all that is changing. I am a big huge fan of Curvy Kate and Panache bras.

JERRY SPRINGER FINAL THOUGHT. I carry a tape measure in my purse. Andy cringes when I pull it out in department stores or on the TSA security lines at the airport. I talk about bras the same way Jehovah's Witnesses show up at your house to remind you there's no hell.

And I am perfectly okay with being the crazy lady who wants to wrap a tape measure around you if it means that you'll feel good about your boobs. Not *wanting* to be a certain bra size is not the same as not *being* that size. I promise you, I will never guess what your bra size is in a well-fitting bra, but I can tell what size you aren't in a bra that doesn't fit. (Please also apply this anecdote to jeans, bodycon dresses, leggings, and mouth retainers.)

CHAPTER 5

If These Spanx Could Talk

A few years back, Andy and I were invited to the wedding of one of his college friends. The affair was to be held at a sailing club in Chicago. Faaaancy! This was underscored by the fact that it was an adults-only reception, which I know can get a little dicey for people who believe children should be invited everywhere, but we are not those people, and happily chest-bumped at the thought of a weekend alone in a hotel, drinking to excess and not being in charge of cutting up anyone else's meat.

It was also one of those situations where Andy was asked to be a member of the wedding, but I was not, and that was totally fine. I didn't really know the bride very well, and the fewer bridesmaid dresses in my life, the better, as you can probably guess. It was, however, a black-tie event. Faaaaancy! As such, it was not the type of event we normally find ourselves attending.

I purchased a black satin trumpet-cut gown for this swank shindig, and due to the thinness of the fabric, I knew I would need some serious shape wear. I typically avoid such torture in the summer, as my body temperature runs hot and I turn into a big wet heat rash.

Also, shape wear sometimes makes me feel a little trapped and claustrophobic and my stomach skin gets all, *"If I don't exhale and stretch all the way out right this second, I'm going to fucking lose it. I swear to God, Brittany, get me out of this elastic coffin or I will fucking kill you and everyone around you."*

Listen, I know some people have really strong feelings about shape wear. First there are angry dudes on the Internet who say women who wear Spanx are somehow cheating or deceiving them. As if women are tricking men into liking them by reshaping their bodies. This just speaks to a general misunderstanding about what foundation garments are, and the failure to understand such concepts as object permanence. Women aren't changing their bodies with Spanx—it's not liposuction. For me, Spanx are the difference between having smooth fat or visible panty-line fat. Those are the choices I get; none of the choices are Kate Moss.

Shape wear is often panned by some women as the antithesis of body positivity. And there are valid points to their arguments. You shouldn't ever feel that your body has to look or behave a certain way in order to be beautiful. Almost all women-targeted marketing is done through the promise of weight loss or beauty. And Spanx and corsets are great ways to swing your body pendulum toward a more normalized beauty standard.

Can you be body positive and wear shape wear? Um, yeah, I think so. Loving your body is about being comfortable in your body, and only you get to set the parameters of that, only you get to decide what it looks like, and only you know where your finish line is. Never let anyone make you feel ashamed about what you decide, or don't decide, to put onto your body. If you feel like you're beautiful only when you wear shape wear, I'd say we have some work to do. But if you wear Spanx because you like them, and like yourself just as much when you don't, carry on, my wayward sister!

So, as I was saying, I decided to wear Spanx to smooth out the beautiful lines of the trumpet gown, and in this instance, Spanx is plural, as in, I wore two pair. (I wanted to clarify that, because the plural of Spanx is Spanx . . . like deer or moose, so it can be confusing.)

The first layer looked like giant briefs, which, if we're being honest, is a typical Brittany move; I like to wear things that make me feel held in, because this makes me feel safe and comfortable. I wear many garments pulled up to my retinas—jeans, skirts, period underwear—so these granny panties Spanx are really not outside my wheelhouse. Then over that, I layered a pair of tummy/thigh combo Spanx.

I don't know the technical term, so I refer to those as the "half-wrestling-singlet variety."

The first ten minutes of being dressed is the best and most effective the shape wear will ever react to my body. The second I have to sit down, it's like a slow, painful prison escape to the floor for these bitches.

> *To the window, to the wall!*
> *Til the sweat drop down my balls*
> *Til all these bitches crawl . . .*

Yes, that's right, Lil Jon was rapping about wearing Spanx in the summer the whole time.

Six hours later, the wedding was over and we climbed out of a taxi and took the elevator to our room on the thirty-fifth floor overlooking Navy Pier. As I explained earlier, our general rule is that if we are away from our kids, we have sex, unless we're away doing something where that would be frowned on, like going to prison or lying in a hospital bed giving birth to a baby. Otherwise, even if we are tired or grumpy, we try to make it a point to take advantage of our time alone. It'd be like going to Memphis and not visiting Graceland.

"What is happening under here?" Andy asked, unzipping my gown while I pulled the fake lashes from my eyelids.

Normally, I would not handle my shape-wear business in front of him. We don't have many secrets between us, but some things are worth being left unseen to keep the mystery alive, and putting on shape wear is one of those things. Nobody wants to know how the sausage gets made. Especially since one of the names I use for shape wear is "sausage casing."

"How do I get this off?" he asked, confused about what tube to attack first.

"Don't worry about it." I kissed him as we fell back onto the king-size bed.

Spanx, the brand-name kind anyway, come conveniently equipped with an open hole in the crotch for easier bathroom access. The idea is that you don't have to pull your Spanx off, you can just squat and pee through the existing hole. If you are wearing any other brand of shape wear, it's really easy to take a pair of scissors and DIY that little slit yourself. Just don't get too aggressive with your cutting; it's all too easy to go from shape wear to assless chaps.

In my opinion, the brand-name pee hole is a little on the small side, so while that makes for tricky aim, especially when you're drinking, it does make me feel a little bit tighter when it counts, if you know what I'm saying . . .

In the heat of the moment, Andy noticed nothing, he was far too distracted by my boobs and the pretty bra and the fact that we could hump to our hearts' content without little fists banging on our bedroom door, and us having to yell, "Go away, we're on the phone with Santa!"

After we finished, Andy ordered hamburgers and fries from room service, and joined me lying quietly on the still-made bed, looking out the wall-length window at the colored lights on the water.

All at once it all became too much.

"You have to get these off of me," I gasped, feeling suddenly light-headed and trapped.

I clawed at the spandex while Andy dug through my purse for tools. A few moments later he pushed me back, and using the emergency corkscrew I keep in my bag at all times, tore through the two layers of shape wear, and peeled the moist black scuba suit from my body.

I filled my lungs to capacity for the first time since being seated on the groom's side at three o'clock sharp.

"It burns. It burns so good."

It was like baptism by shape wear, and I emerged from the water born again and with this weird *linea nigra* from the tummy seam.

But, I have to say . . . the sex was kinda worth it.

Not everything I wear under my clothes is made of spandex and serves the sole purpose of a foundational torture. Yes, due to my size, support is needed, but sometimes I just want to wear something so sexy it gets me instantaneously bent over a bed. Or a desk. Or the inside of an elevator.

Up until very recently, plus-size undergarments were made for comfort, not seduction. The "sexy" lingerie we were offered came from twenty-four-hour adult stores right off the exits of major interstates. It came in plastic costume bags generically labeled PLUS SIZE, and all of it reflected some sort of fetish or sexual role.

Being a sexy nurse is fine on Halloween, but on a Tuesday in March, I want to be the sexy adult, author, and businesswoman I am, no costume needed. Curvy women weren't getting the message that they could just be sexy as themselves, and not have to pretend to be someone else entirely.

Don't get me wrong, I am not at all against role-playing, Andy and I often role-play during our date nights, pretending to be two strangers meeting for the first time after connecting on Tinder. He plays a single British businessman with a strong affection for dogs who's only in the country for a week. I'm Sheryl Sandberg ready to lean into a good time. It gets pretty steamy.

But under normal circumstances, I just want to wear something that makes me feel gorgeous and romantic, and that can look different for everybody.

Confession, I have never seen *The Notebook,* and I've only seen the first half of *Titanic.* I'm going to assume everything turns out fine for both couples.

But if Jack were to paint my portrait in the parking area of a doomed cruise ship, I wouldn't be naked. Lying on my side can cause my boobs to get a little too "Picasso" when left to gravity. Instead I'd be wearing a lavender lace bra under a thinning white V-neck T-shirt and matching lavender lace boy shorts with my hair tossed up in a ponytail.

That right there is my sex outfit. My "leave-the-lights-on, you're-definitively-getting-laid, head-cocked-to-the-side, bottom-lip-nibbling" sex outfit.

The sexiest women I know are sexy because they feel sexy for themselves *first*. I spent far too much of my life trying to make myself desirable for someone else and, in so doing, allowing that person to enjoy my body more than I enjoyed my body. I put on tank tops with built-in bras and covered my body with duvets. Sex was sweaty and hot because I hid shamefully under a blanket in the middle of summer, not because I was enjoying it and it was erotically aerobic. I lay on a bed, and while he moaned with pleasure, I focused on keeping my legs flexed enough so they wouldn't jiggle. When I got onto my knees I asked him to go slower so that my ass didn't slap so loudly against him. And when I rolled onto my side, I grabbed the pillow from behind my head and squeezed it to hide my stomach.

Being sexy for my husband wasn't working for him because it would have required a miner's hat to actually see me in the dark, and it wasn't working for me because I wasn't present enough to enjoy it anyways. Not with all the flappy and sticking and slapping noises and trying to control everything.

Andy telling me he thought I was sexy wasn't working, because I didn't believe him, and then it hurt his feelings that I didn't believe him, so then I was apologizing for not believing him, which is an asinine thing to have to apologize for, and what the hell was happening?

I remember thinking, *I don't want to die, go to heaven, and when St. Peter asks me if I had fun, have my answer be, "No, but I tried really hard to make sure everyone else did."* As women, we are raised to be selfless beings. It's why our dinners are always cold when we finally sit down to eat. Or more accurately, stand over the counter and shovel our food in after everyone else leaves the kitchen.

Your priority in this life is you. Yes, keep the kids alive, and be a great partner in your relationships, but none of that should come at the expense of you. And for me in the bedroom, it most certainly was. Even after I got my life back outside the bedroom.

Here's the thing—you don't need to lower the bar, and in fact, you shouldn't. You need to realize that you are the one who holds the bar to begin with. Being sexy and comfortable are not mutually exclusive.

I'm not telling you to spend the rest of your life in sweatpants, but I don't think we're giving the people in our lives, or ourselves, enough credit if we assume the only way anyone will want us is if we stop looking like we actually enjoy being ourselves. The road to sexy starts with one step.

My first step was buying some decent drawers. I looked in my underwear drawer and realized how atrocious my underwear supply had gotten. I've worn swimsuit bottoms to gynecologist appointments because I hadn't bought underwear since before having children. Now I know that all my doctor does is look at vaginas all day, and I'm sure she's seen some doozies, but I was ashamed to let her see the sad state of my undergarments: high-rise maternity under- wear that had faded to almost nothing, elastic coming through at the waist and leg holes, and fully stained from heavy period use.

It's really hard to feel sexy when you look like a nursing- home patient. It's just that underwear had always been a low-priority purchase for me. My kids always needed some- thing more than I needed cute panties.

So during the dark drawer days, I went to the theater with friends to see *Fifty Shades of Grey,* and of course bought a giant bin of popcorn, even though the older I get, the less my bowels enjoy it. Seriously, I can't say no to it, yet can't make it through a movie without violently shooting that salty business back out of my body.

All of a sudden there was a point in the movie, about the halfway mark on my popcorn bucket, when I laughed so hard that I pooped my pants. Not a ton, but enough for it to be the type of emergency you address right away.

I remember reading that some cinema chains purchased plastic seat covers for their theaters because they thought the movie would turn so many women on they'd simulta- neously ejaculate. Perhaps they should also have planned for laughter-induced popcorn shits.

When I got to the restroom, I simply cleaned myself off and tossed my underwear in the garbage, no second thoughts given. After the movie, I recounted the hilari- ous story to my friends and they were horrified, not that

I'd pooped my pants, we've all been there, but that I'd just tossed my underwear away.

"Why wouldn't you wrap it up and put it in your purse?" Meredith asked. "You don't throw away good underwear."

They all nodded in agreement, and then I explained that I didn't have good underwear. Just the threadbare kangaroo-pouch-looking stuff from when I was pregnant, and I realized then that my friends probably wore this thing known as gooooood underwear. Grown-ass women need grown-ass underwear, and I had totally missed the boat on this.

I now have two underwear drawers. The first, comprising more everyday options, includes sleek black bikini cuts, some higher-rise briefs that make me feel held in under dresses, and my official "period underwear." Which is no longer old underwear with stains on it, but rather more expensive investment pieces of Thinx that are lined with magic and hold entire tampons' worth of blood. Seriously, what are those things made of?

My second drawer is full of satin and lace, the kind of underwear you wear when you need to know that underneath your clothes you're pure sex and strength. What this drawer lacks in breathability and natural fibers, it makes up for in confidence and fun. Let's just say that I don't wear anything from this drawer to church. Not because of Jesus, but because they don't have air-conditioning in the house of the Lord, and between the sweat and the satin, I'd slide right off the pew.

I now have sex with the lights on. Not just because my underwear is sexy, but because treating myself to things that make me feel sexy and cared for makes me feel like I am worth feeling sexy and cared for, and I am.

Also, nobody should be wearing a thirty-dollar pair of panties in the dark.

CHAPTER 6

I'm Getting Married; Suck It, Julia Roberts

Andy weighs eighty pounds less than I do. If my life were a television show, he would be married to my best friend. He and I would know each other, of course. We'd probably meet at a bar while I was out with my girlfriends, and when the thinner one went to the bathroom, he'd call me over to get to know me. And while he asked about my job and where I was from, my heart would flutter a little bit.

Oh my God, he asked me to sit next to him, and now our forearms are touching on the bar.

Then Andy would ask me if my friend and I needed a drink, or if we were friends from work. When she came out of the bathroom, he'd ask us if we wanted to join him and his friend in a game of pool. I'd say yes right away, dragging my gorgeous bestie along, and Andy and I would trade banter all night, playfully brushing against each other as we took turns taking shots. And then at the end of the night, I'd stall a bit getting my coat on, and when he walked over to us nervously, my heart would stop. And then he'd ask my best friend out on a date.

I'd probably be in their wedding, getting paired with one of the bride's chubby male cousins, and I'd make a hilarious toast. I'd go on to be their children's godparent and around for all their holiday celebrations, where they'd put their arms around each other across the counter from me and say, "If only a guy could see what a catch you are, Brittany." And they'd shake their heads.

I don't look like the girl who gets the guy, at least not as far as romantic comedies and network sitcoms go. And when that's the only message you're getting, it's really hard not to believe it. You can't help but think you're only good enough to be cast in the role of supporting actress/supportive best friend.

Sure, pretty friend, let me help you meet the man of your dreams.

Come to my house when you're fighting with your hot spouse and drink my wine and explain to me why I don't understand what your feelings feel like.

By all means, feel free to fix me up with the heavyset man in your office.

When I text you a photo of what I'm wearing on our first date, tell me I look sassy, and that we make an "adorable" couple.

And when I get married, treat it with the same maturity you showed when planning your dog's birthday party. After all, chubby-best-friend roles don't "get" passion or sexuality. We are just feel-good one-dimensional cartoons acting as wing women so you can freely flirt with men at the bar or on the dance floor.

You are Julia Roberts and I am Rebel Wilson, and everyone knows the movie ends when Julia Roberts gets the guy.

I met Andy when I was fifteen years old. He had gotten into a car accident in front of my house, asked to use my phone, and he never left. Seriously, I could not get this kid to stop coming over.

Andy was tall and thin; he played basketball and golf, listened to rap music, and came from a family with money. I was chubby, poor, and hated when people came over to my house because my mom bred cocker spaniels and all of our chewed-up furniture smelled like dogs and was covered in fur.

I even pretended to sleep in on the weekends so he'd go away, but my mom just let him in the house and sent him back to my bedroom, where he'd sit on the corner of my bed, dogs piled on top of him, waiting for me to wake up.

What the hell, Mom! Haven't you ever seen any of the Lifetime movies where thirty-year-old Kellie Martin plays some teenager that was attacked by the otherwise unassuming high school jock?

His attention was a severe mental adjustment for me. I

was so used to obsessing over boys who would never actually date me that I didn't know how to process Andy and his persistence, undeterred by my fake narcolepsy and bed head.

I mean, you read the second chapter; I wore JNCO jeans that were made for a boy, for fuck's sake. What was I to do with a boy who just liked me, the Nominee for Best Supporting Actress?

I think one of the reasons I have such a strong relationship with Andy Gibbons* is because I learned how to actually like and accept myself right beside him and his insistence on liking and accepting me just the way I was. In fact, I don't think I have ever had to hide something about me or pretend to like something he liked out of insecurity.

I am a terrible golfer because I have boobs and struggle with figuring out the difference between swinging a bat and swinging a golf club, so that's out. I couldn't fit into his basketball jersey in high school, so he never pressured me to wear it. We both worked through college, so money was never really a huge issue. I mean, yeah, I have done absolutely nothing to trick this boy into liking me.

Actually, that's not entirely true. I did, briefly, pretend to like Guinness to impress him. It was his favorite beer at the time, and whenever he mentioned it, I knowingly nodded my head in agreement.

Like yeah, I'm Irish, obviously I like Guinness.

---

*So help me God, Andy Gibbons, if you divorce me for any reason after the publication of this book, I will never forgive you, and if I die first, I will haunt you.

One night during college we met some friends at a bar, and while I was in the bathroom, he ordered me a pint of Guinness, like the gentleman that he is. It was thick, frothy, and disgusting, and I choked it down, sip by painful sip. It was, to date, my greatest performance. The car ride home was long and warm, and every coffee-flavored burp brought me dangerously close to losing it, until eventually, I leaned my head out the window and vomited dark brown ale down the side of his car and into the open window slot.

From then on, that car smelled like puke every time you opened the window. That was officially the last time I pretended to like something for a boy.

Andy asked me to marry him when we were twenty-three years old, in the dark . . . in a cemetery. I didn't even know you were allowed inside cemeteries after dark, but apparently you can make arrangements for such a thing with the creepy guy who digs the graves.

At the time of our engagement, I was working as a wedding planner for a prestigious local golf club. It was a high-pressure job with horrible hours and emotional brides that had the capability to treat you very badly in the name of stress and anxiety. I didn't blame them, weddings can be terrible. They cost a lot of money, they take a long time to plan, and without fail, they almost always result in family drama or loss of friendships. I planned the nuptials of beautiful women with unlimited budgets, and I can assure you that under the best financial and relationship circumstances, weddings turn people into awful flaming garbage monsters.

There was no scenario in which getting married wasn't going to be horrible. It was for this reason that I begged Andy to elope. He said no.

I wasn't always a jaded, grumpy wedding hater. Once my mother backed away from working as a buyer for my grandmother's bridal salon, she took over doing the books and inventory in a small office above the showroom. On Fridays after school, I would sit at the alteration tables upstairs and listen to the old Greek women laugh and gossip as they sewed intricate beading to white silk and lace. They paused every few minutes, assessing the work I'd been doing stitching spare buttons onto scrap pieces of elastic, and cooed my name approvingly into three thick syllables.

"That looks good, Breet-tan-neee."

I loved nothing more than tiptoeing through the fitting areas, sneaking glimpses of gushing brides being fawned over by their eager mothers and best friends. They'd catch their reflection in the mirror and sigh, and you just knew it was the very first moment they felt like a bride.

After the shop closed for the night, I put on long lace veils and marched up and down the staircase through the center of the showroom, smiling appreciatively at the well-dressed mannequins who lined my procession, finally stopping at the top of the steps and turning to meet my groom, who, for the majority of fifth grade, was Bill Murray from *Ghostbusters*. That's right, Mom, I was going to marry a doctor.

Eventually, my grandmother got cancer and was forced to sell the shop. It was heartbreaking. Every dreamy feeling I had about getting married came from those halls, and I always assumed that one day I would be standing in that shop, wearing a wedding dress of my own.

When Andy and I told my parents we were getting married, long after the shop had closed and my grandmother passed away, my mom ran out of the room and returned carrying a big beautiful white box. There, underneath the yellowed tissue paper, was a champagne-colored silk gown with long sleeves and a beaded bow on each shoulder. It was a dress that my grandmother had saved for me from her store to wear on my wedding day.

It was also a size 8.

God bless my bridal-shop-owning grandmother, Jeanne Erausquin, but the last time I had been a size 8 was at my preschool graduation.

I spent the next week tracking down one of the few living Greek seamstresses from the shop, Angela, and desperately shoved the dress into her frail hands, pleading with her to make it fit my body as beautifully as the gowns she'd sewn in the past.

She wore all black, having lost her husband a few months prior, and tearfully shook her head no when I invited her to the wedding. She was still mourning her beloved Peter, and wasn't attending any social events for the rest of the year.

She stood well below my shoulders as she buzzed around

me taking my measurements and scratching numbers onto a small scrap of paper.

She then laid the yellowed gown down across her cleared kitchen table, turning the skirt inside out and pulling at the seams of the bodice, and after I watched her work for about ten minutes, she gently folded the dress back into the box, pressed it into my hands, and shook her head.

"No," she announced.

"But what if we—"

"No." She cut me off. "You are too big."

She smiled warmly and waved from the porch as I walked out of her house, opened the trunk of my car, and shoved the package in with the nonchalance that a dress with nothing more than sentimental associations deserved.

For the wedding that I didn't want, to the man I desperately loved but still wasn't sure I was supposed to get, I realized I would have to endure the unthinkable. I would have to go wedding-dress shopping.

Even though I understood bridal sizing was the work of the devil and most shops offered a very limited inventory of plus-size gowns, I was still totally blindsided by how dehumanizing and difficult the process actually was.

I'd arrived at my appointment with my mother and maid of honor, wearing every single piece of shape wear I owned. It was like a torture expert had forced three hundred rubber bands around a watermelon.

The bridal shop in question had none of the personal magic of my grandmother's, and instead was just rows and

rows of small stalls that opened up to a large shared mirror. It was like a slaughterhouse, but with tulle. My attendant, Michelle, wore a tight black suit with scuffed-up black
heels; she had black drawn-on eyebrows and a face that
looked positively exhausted at our 11 A.M. arrival. She told
me I could select up to four gowns to try on, all of them the
standard sample size of 8 or 10, and to let her know when
I'd found something I liked. And then she disappeared into
a back room, to silent-scream, I guess.

This was supposed to be a major life event with all the
quirky romance and humor of a Nora Ephron movie. I was
a bride searching for my wedding gown; where was the
champagne, girl talk, and upbeat female-themed ukulele
music?

The reality is that there is nothing at all rom-com about
waddling out of a dressing room as a size 18 woman with
a size 10 dress chip-clipped to the front of your body like a
paper doll.

The thinner women around me burst out of their rooms
like Disney princesses, spinning around and beaming at their
smiling entourage of supporters. When I stood in front of the
three-way mirror, it was like I had a tiny dress floating on the
front of my body, and the back was just a sea of nude-colored
Spanx and back fat. There was no spinning or twirling, just
my mom and Michelle, biting the insides of their cheeks and
turning their heads curiously to the side in consideration.

"Imagine this dress coming down the aisle," I explained,
"but with my actual human body inside it."

I fell in love with a champagne lace ball gown reminiscent of Grace Kelly, and I had to order it ten sizes larger than the sample, a task to be completed, might I add, without my ever actually trying it on. I don't even decide on ice cream at Cold Stone without trying at least five different samples, but here I was, spending over a thousand dollars on a dress that I had never been inside of.

Seven months is a long time to wait for that "Oh my God, I'm really a bride" moment. But that is how long it took for the dress to arrive from the designer, and when I finally put it on and it fit—even a little loosely moreover— it was one of the happiest moments of my life. Even Michelle wiped sweat from her forehead in relief, taking one of her eyebrows right off with it, and joined me in the absolute excitement of being just another normal, blissfully happy bride in a dress.

All brides deserve this moment, and yet there are very few things in life as defeating as wedding-dress shopping for someone over size 14. Maybe joining an adult dodgeball league? That was unexpectedly violent. But dress shopping definitely ranks right up there with it.

I am officially the last person my friends call to tell me they are engaged, not because they don't like me, but because I've been known to scream things like "don't do it, weddings are stupid!"

I remember waking up the morning after Andy and

my wedding extravaganza and realizing just how much money we'd spent the night before, and how little we had to show for it. I mean, yes, we had a marriage, but that part cost only a hundred dollars. Everything else we'd paid tens of thousands for was now only tangible in photos; the Rat Pack impersonators, the Chinese takeout buffet, the dark red rose centerpieces . . . all of it consumed and gone by morning.

I've never asked Andy if he regrets having had a big wedding, though he's the one who'd pressed for it. Andy's brother, Jason, is nine years older than he is, making Andy the fifteen-year-old best man at his wedding in 1996. Since then, he'd always been desperate to replicate the same type of lavish affair. In his mind, by doing so he'd make his parents proud. I've long suspected some *Brady Bunch*–level jealousy there, but Andy insists that there is none.

Sure, Jan.

The compromise to this two-hundred-guest blowout at home in Ohio, Andy promised me that the next year we would fly to Vegas with some of our best friends and re-new our vows in front of Elvis. Which was *my* version of a dream wedding.

The problem with this plan was that it never happened, because Andy kept knocking me up. For five years I was either pregnant, breastfeeding, or nursing a fresh set of epi-siotomy stiches, keeping me from the wedding I had been promised. I mean, I guess I could have gone between ba-bies, but who wants to go to Vegas to get hitched while their nipples are leaking?

Then, six years ago, seven years after our first wedding, Andy and I were sitting in LaGuardia Airport at 4 A.M. waiting for a Dunkin' Donuts to open. I'd flown in to New York to host a women's event with Gavin DeGraw, and Andy tagged along for company.

It'd been a pretty grueling turnaround, with a late-night concert and then an early-morning flight, but when you have three small kids, you almost never turn down the chance to sleep on clean white sheets or to have sex in a bed without the fear of someone banging on your door.

As I sat across from a coffee machine, mentally willing the darkened kiosk to open, Andy turned to me and kissed me, and before I could realize what was happening, he knelt on the floor in front of a rabbi and the guy running the vacuum in the gate area next to us, and he asked me to marry him, again.

This time around, the wedding happened on my terms. I booked a campy boutique hotel in Las Vegas that streamed complimentary eighties porn in every room, which is actually my favorite kind of pornography. It's sexy seeing normal people with overbites and bushes of hair all over their bodies, instead of the barely legal robot porn you can watch on the Internet these days.

I invited all my most fun friends, planned burlesque bachelorette parties for the girls, and booked gambling and golfing for Andy and his boys.

And when it came to the dress, I threw every fat-girl fashion rule out the window and ordered a white tulle vintage Marilyn Monroe gown cut clear down to my belly button, which, after three kids, sits far lower than it would have for my first trip down the aisle. There were no dressing room indignities. There was no waiting seven months, no princess fantasy bullshit. I wore what made me feel like the hot, sexy wife I was, for the man who I knew was waiting for me at the end of the aisle and who I knew was going to be thrilled to take that dress off me at the end of that super-fun night.

Andy and I were married under the neon Vegas lights by a hairy-chested Elvis in a white bejeweled jumpsuit, promising not be a hound dog and to love each other tender, until death do us part.

It's so easy to forget, in the tsunami that is planning, that a wedding is inherently only supposed to be about the two of you. It's about marrying someone you love, with even more people you love around you, showing them just how awesome it is when two of their favorite people join together.

And that can look however you want it to look, at whatever dress size you are, with whomever you choose to love. You are not stuck in a rom-com as a third-wheel sidekick to anyone else's happy ending (read, Julia Roberts's fat friend). Every part of your story is the important part; from the engagement, to dress, to the vows. There is a lid for every pot, a match for every sock. Even chubby girls get the guy. The hot one, too.

I can't talk about weddings without bringing up the dreaded issue of bridesmaiding and bridesmaid dresses. Especially since I can now be all Yoda and reflective about this, as most of my friends are past the wedding stage of their lives and have moved on to babies or divorce parties—two stages I find to be infinitely easier to shop for. Bibs or vibrators, it's so simple.

A few pounds of flesh are always demanded anytime you accept the honor of being a bridesmaid. You agree to help the bride with the planning, to help throw the shower and tag along for any prewedding appointments where your support is needed, and lastly, you agree to walk down the aisle and wear the dress.

Every time I've been asked, I always frantically scream "yes!" as being chosen and important is exciting. Who's special? I'm special. Sorry, lady handing out programs, you didn't make the cut.

And then that enthusiasm starts to wane as soon as my bride-to-be friend calls and she only wants to talk about how her future mother-in-law wants to wear white, and the caterer didn't have the right shape of chicken, or about how stressful her life is, and I realize that I've signed up to be an indentured servant to a temporarily narcissistic bride zombie who only reaches out to me when she needs something and all the other bridesmaids have started screening her calls. I have to listen to all of this, mind you, while also agreeing to buy and wear the dress.

A dress I have very little input in selecting and purchasing at a price point I cannot control. Let me just say this: I love my friends very much and have been honored to stand beside them in their amazing weddings. But let me also say this: I have never worn a bridesmaid dress I felt beautiful in. I've never worn a bridesmaid dress I felt confident in. And I've never worn a bridesmaid dress twice. That whole "you can wear it again" thing.

Totally.

Made.

Up.

Now, I am not above criticism myself here. The dresses for my wedding were strapless and cost over $150, and I rationalized all that away by reminding my bridesmaids that they were black vintage-cut gowns they could totally get a lot of wear out of in the future.

But as brides, they fail, I think, to understand one thing. Bridesmaids are people standing up beside you; we are not props, eye candy, or Pinterest projects. We are your foundation for this next big step in your life. We are the people you are going to call to catch up with when you get back from your honeymoon, and celebrate with when you buy a new house, or decide to become parents, or get that amazing new job. We are your people. Show us the respect we deserve, and let us feel confident and comfortable supporting you on your biggest day.

Also, I mean, we're going to be the ones holding your dress for you every time you have to pee. Be nice to us. As such, I thought I'd share some rules. Feel free to make copies and pass them along to your newly engaged friends.

7 Rules for Not Being an
Asshole to the Fat Bridesmaid

1. Do not ask her to lose weight for your wedding. If she wants to on her own accord, fine, I guess. But that is not a logical demand you get to make of another human. You are her friend and the bride, not the casting director for the movie *Black Swan*.

2. Just decide on a color and let the girls pick out their own dresses. This is totally a fun trend right now, and it's a great way to make sure that every girl is wearing a dress she loves.

3. If you don't want to let each girl pick out her own dress, then let the biggest person in your bridal party have the biggest input. It is not fun to find out, in front of everyone at the bridal salon, that the dress the smaller girls picked out does not come in a size big enough for the largest girl.

4. Do not put her in a different dress from the rest of the bridal party. This does not feel special, it feels like an afterthought, an accommodation, or that we're too fat for the normal dresses, which we are, and you don't need to highlight this for the entire guest list.

5. Consider the alterations. I have no doubt your friend is willing and excited to buy in to your big day, but try to remember that oftentimes it will be at a larger expense than smaller members of

your party. Plus-size dresses not only sometimes cost more, they are also pricier to alter, and might require super-expensive undergarments.

6. Do not automatically make her walk with the only fat groomsman. Size doesn't bond people the way an obsession with *Game of Thrones* does.

7. And lastly, please don't do any of those group pictures where everyone has to jump in the air at the same time. It's incredibly unflattering to 98 percent of the population, the exception being small children or dogs catching Frisbees.

CHAPTER 7

Brittany with the Good Hair

"Is that your natural hair color?"

I'd like to take a moment to go over some rules I have regarding hair, specifically, when it is and isn't appropriate to ask someone if they dye theirs.

Situations wherein it's completely okay to ask me if I dye my hair:

1. You are performing some sort of beauty process on me, making the environment fitting to discuss intimate matters about my beauty regime.
2. We're in the bathroom of a bar, and you're holding my hair back while I throw up all the sugary umbrella drinks I shouldn't have downed.

3. You are a homicide detective and you are at my door holding a hair that you found at the scene of the crime.

4. I'm channeling Effie Trinket and my hair is an unnatural color, such as pink or blue or green.

Situations wherein it's absolutely not okay to ask me if I dye my hair:

When I am out somewhere in public and you get the hankering to inquire about my hair in front of my husband or just about anyone else on the planet.

It's not that it's a secret or that my own husband doesn't know that I dye my hair, but honestly, you and I don't know each other. For all you know, you could be outing my number one confidence booster in front of a first date or potential boss. Why don't you ask me if I stuff my bra or whether I had a nose job? The answer to both is no, by the way. The stuff in my bra isn't for enhancement; it's for survival should I get trapped in an emergency situation and need sustenance from the Skittles and popcorn trapped in there.

Once, I was sitting in an Outback Steakhouse with my husband and a group of his international coworkers that I was meeting for the first time, and our server set down a few loaves of bread, turned to me, and loudly asked, "Oh my God, is your hair real or fake?"

"It's a better version of what comes out of my head." I

smiled. This has become my canned response in these instances.

I was incredibly flattered to learn that she loved my hair, and I do love me some girl talk, but asking me in front of a table full of people isn't the time. Instead, pull me aside when I am going to the bathroom for the ninth time, or stop me when we're leaving.

I know this sounds a little blown out of proportion and you are probably thinking, *But Brittany, it's just hair?* And it is, I know, but as a fat girl, I'm ridiculously protective of my locks, and have been all my life. I had to be, I grew up believing it was all I had going for me and that it was my only beauty qualifier.

Fat girls give good hair and have pretty faces. We've heard it a million times.

I was very blessed to have two aunts in my family who were amazing hair stylists, and it's from them I learned not only how to take care of my mane, but how I could use it as an access point for laying down a personal style.

From junior high on, I spent an extraordinary amount of time in these hair wizards' salon chairs. Glossing over the various poorly chosen perms I requested, I'm going to confidently call it: I had one of the best heads of hair in my school. My thick waves were a great foundation for withstanding all the bleaching, coloring, and hacking into them we did on a monthly basis.

I had short messy layers like Drew Barrymore in *Mad Love,* nineties baby bangs like Janeane Garofalo in *Reality*

Bites, and long curly red hair like Marissa Ribisi in the box-office smash *The Brady Bunch Movie.* I was a chameleon and I loved that. I may not have been able to express my personality as effectively as I wanted with fashion, but hair always fits.

So to answer your question, I wasn't always a redhead. Just sometimes.

I first dyed my hair copper-red in junior high school. I was so excited to surprise my then boyfriend, Vince. But when I walked up behind him and put my arms around his waist, he turned around, backed away, and asked me why I looked like Peg Bundy. He and the friend he was with erupted in laughter.

Not really what you want to hear from the guy who fingers you in the back of the theater during *Lethal Weapon,* at least not at the time. Now that I'm older I realize Peg Bundy had a bangin' body and great hair. Thirty-six-year-old Brittany would high-five her boyfriend for the comment. She would also then promptly break up with him because she doesn't date guys who don't clean under their fingernails and try to make her feel bad about her hair.

I may have been born a dirty blonde, but being a ginger is in my blood. My grandmother had gorgeous auburn hair. I remember watching her lose it in her hands as she went through chemotherapy, hiding her emerging scalp beneath colorful scarves and wraps. It's one of those odd things you often think about when someone passes away. I miss my grandma's hair, and the smell of her brand of shampoo.

I didn't stay red for long in junior high, quickly cycling through ever-lighter shades of platinum blond to offset my darker eyebrows, which I plucked into thin, reclining commas. Bleach-blond hair was the language of teenagers in the late nineties and early two thousands. Girls showed off the chunky highlights made popular by denim-clad superstars who marched their way down an MTV red carpet, and frosted tips were a dreamy-boy-band calling card. We were on the wrong side of hair history, and I'm not proud of it.

On any normal day, I estimate Andy to give less than two shits about my hair, and I am completely okay with that. I can come home from the salon and he may or may not notice, and that's fine. The only reason I know when he trims his beard is because he leaves all the hair in the sink like a molting bird.

I think we are both really good about knowing what the other likes, and live by a general set of rules we laid out on our wedding night. Vows, if you will. Honestly, we were too drunk and exhausted to consummate our new marriage, so we just collapsed on our bed fully dressed and wrote out silly promises to each other until we had to leave for the airport and catch the flight to our honeymoon.

"Promise me we'll always want to have sex with one another," he wrote.

"Promise me you'll always think I'm the funniest girl you know."

"Promise me you'll never make me sell my car for a minivan."

We went back and forth laughing, completely unaware that you can't accurately make these sorts of predictions when you are twenty-three years old with no children or debt.

"Promise me you'll never ask me if I really need to order two eggrolls," I wrote.

"Promise me you'll never get a short mom haircut," he scribbled in all caps.

"Promise me you'll pretend you don't notice when I poop."

"Promise me you won't use my razor to shave your pubic hair."

Let me tell you . . . that last one? There's probably quite a market for guys in prison who'd be into that sort of thing, and I'd look into it more if you were allowed to mail razors jammed with pubes to inmates. Just sayin'.

To date, we've kept the majority of these promises to each other. Even with three kids, neither of us drives a van and Andy still pretends the bathroom doesn't smell like a lit match when I walk out. However, the razor thing was a deal breaker. Andy's razor is so much sharper than mine, and if it's a choice between ending up with a vagina that looks like Michael Chiklis or Deadpool, I'm choosing Chiklis.

Up until this point, my hair has largely been a nonissue in our relationship. I had been sticking to dark chestnut shades, attempting to look exotic next to Andy's dark skin and black hair, a task I had taken over doing at home with boxed color. This would be mistake number one. I am not made to have dark brown hair. My skin is too fair and the inky hues washed me out and made me look green. This was further confirmed when I caught Andy Photoshopping a tan onto my skin in one of our wedding pictures. This is a man who had previously had a soul patch and wore gold chains with the Nike symbol hanging from them. If *he* was concerned about my grooming choices, something had to be horribly amiss.

The second broken promise happened shortly after the birth of our daughter. Here I was, coming off decades of being on top of my hair game, and then a moment of weakness, exhaustion, and sleep deprivation caused me to do the exact thing I always swore I wouldn't do . . . I got a mom haircut.

I walked into the salon like a zombie; I smelled like spoiled milk and war. My stained nursing top was damp against my chest and my long dark hair was thrown into a knotted ball behind my head. It was obvious that someone who looks like me shouldn't be making long-term decisions. But then everyone is so nice to you at the salon, asking about the baby, squeezing your shoulders in fellowship, massaging your scalp a little extra at the shampoo bowl. I was drunk on pampering and *People* magazines.

I don't remember what happened after that. I just remember standing up, seeing a mountain of hair on the floor, and the stylist escorting me to the desk as she fed me platitudes in her soothing radio DJ voice.

"This is going to save you so much time."

"Your hair is so much healthier now."

"Your baby won't even recognize you."

"It will be so much easier."

The haircut was horrible. I had walked into the salon with hair that fell below my shoulder blades and left with a choppy short bob that sat above my chin; like a Dorothy Hamill with more layers. I could no longer pull it back into a ponytail, it was hard to style in any manner outside of matronly, and it aged me at least a decade. And let's get real, there was nothing "easier" about it. When my hair was long, I could simply braid it or toss it up before leaving the house. Having short hair meant I had to actually style it every day, adding even more time and annoyance to my already struggling self-maintenance routine.

It's because of that cut that I stopped cutting and coloring my hair for four years. I went off the grid and all natural. I looked like the before photo of the people whose friends drag them onto daytime talk shows for offensive ambush makeovers. Those poor souls think they are just headed for some freebies as members of the studio audience. Little do they know Wendy Williams is about to pull them onstage and tell them they look like a cross between Rumpelstiltskin and Cruella de Vil.

A few years ago, I spent a week in New York City shooting the fall plus-size clothing campaign for Lands' End. It was my first "big-deal" photo shoot, and I was brought on as the spokesmodel for the campaign based on the various viral body-positivity movements I'd been launching online. I didn't know anything about modeling outside of what I'd picked up from *America's Next Top Model,* but the experience with Lands' End changed my life. I was able to meet with designers and participate in catalog styling and model fittings. It was the moment when I stopped being a passenger on the plus-size fashion train and became one of its most vocal conductors.

While preparing me for my photo shoot, the stylist blowing out my hair commented, "You have the most dramatic ombré dye job I have ever seen." And I smiled, thanking her in a way that assured her that yes, my ombré hair was totally happening on purpose. But in my head, I was suddenly hyperaware that my hair was no longer reading as natural, but as a fading trend I had somehow slacked my way into.

The spotlight only increased following that shoot. I was approached by more fashion brands, and the more I was thrust into the spotlight, the more insecure I began to feel. Not about my body, but about being forgettable. I was a completely average-looking curvy woman, trying desperately to spread a memorable message about loving your body and reinventing how society sees beauty.

The problem was that once I left the stage or a segment on a morning show would end, a trendy celebrity would come out and nobody would remember the curvy girl with Topanga hair and bad roots.

Much the way I learned that dramatic headlines baited readers to learn about loving themselves—FAT GIRL WEARS BIKINI, CHUBBY WOMAN HAS SEX EVERY DAY FOR A YEAR, PLUS-SIZE LADY STRIPS ON TED STAGE—I realized that having a provocative look would help me stand out and brand my message.

"Brand" feels like a dirty word these days, but let's face it—so many successful people are known for their signature look. Anna Wintour has her chin-length bob, Steve Jobs had his black mock turtlenecks, Elton John has his sunglasses . . . these are things that we see and immediately connect to that person.

I ran through a few scenarios. Maybe I could always wear a sweater with a giant *B* on the front, or wear bright red lipstick. I could try an old English monocle, or maybe I would only appear on television with a parrot. I had options.

I'd read once that Lucille Ball was asked by a movie studio to dye her hair red to make her stand out and be more memorable. Obviously it worked; to this day she's the most famous redhead of all time. Perhaps red hair would make me the most memorable fat girl on the Internet?

When I arrived home from the Land's End shoot in New York, I called up Autum, a stylist friend I'd grown up with.

It was time to start getting my hair done by a professional again, not standing in my bathroom naked, using plastic gloves while rapping along with Nicki Minaj.

Immediately discarding the parrot and monocle ideas, Autum and I started talking seriously about dyeing my hair red with the same fervor a head of state exhibits while deciding to invade a country or a TV fan exhibits when they finally decide to drop cable and go with Netflix for good. Andy was on board from the start, though he had very different ideas about what red would look like.

When I said, "I'm going to dye my hair red," he saw Christina Hendricks, Jessica Rabbit, and Scarlett Johannson in *Black Widow,* while I was envisioning Lucy, Anne Shirley, and Angela Chase from *My So-Called Life.*

I think I landed somewhere in the middle.

I don't want to be overly dramatic here, but dyeing my hair red changed my life. Red hair took me from being just a blogger to being a full-time working woman's advocate and fashion spokesmodel. I stood out, I was memorable, and more and more people paid attention to what I had to say. Everyone loves a redhead.

Except for the people who believe they have no souls or want to make magic from their bones.

So the hair on your head isn't your only hair. Yeah, I'm going there. I mean, why not be extra thorough? Pubic hair requires upkeep, too.

My struggles began early.

Once I hit high school, all my friends were actively trimming themselves, but I couldn't quite figure out a way to get the job done discreetly. If I shaved, it took close to an hour, causing the hot water to run out before I could rinse all the hair off my legs, the side of the tub, and the bar of soap. I had to secretly throw entire bars of soap away, leaving my dad to get into the shower and scream, "Who the hell keeps eating the soap?"

Of the various awesome things to come out of the nineties, Nad's had to be one of the strangest. Nad's was a product invented by a woman in Australia for her hairy daughters, and there was an hourlong infomercial for it that ran nightly explaining that you simply spread the heatless wax goo on any hair you wanted to remove, gave it a pull, and the hair was gone.

A jar of it was relatively inexpensive, and one day in an aisle of Walmart, I talked my mom into buying one for me, explaining that I wanted to use it for my upper lip.

Once I was safely back in my locked bedroom, I spread the green wax across the front of my pubic area, laid a cloth strip across the wax, and pulled. It was horrifyingly painful and not at all effective. I tried scraping it, rinsing it with steaming-hot water, blowing it with a hairdryer on high . . . nothing could get the wax off, and for days it stuck there, causing my underwear to further seal it to my skin, eventually working as a junk drawer collecting lint and loose change.

It took a week for the Nad's to become hard enough to start coming off in tiny balls, and I swore I'd never wax again.

From that point on, I resigned myself to life as a shaver. It was easier, cheaper, and I could do it myself, which is typically how I like to address my vulva outside of an intercourse or baby-coming-outta-it setting. For those things, I've found the involvement of others is best.

Technically, life should have gone along well enough after that. I'd do one big shave, and then do maintenance to keep things manageable. But that never happened, as I was simply too lazy. Every shave was the "big" shave, and I would exit the now freezing-cold forty-minute-long shower covered in chunks of hair like a Sasquatch with tennis elbow.

Once I got to adulthood, so many of my friends embraced waxing that I became curious, but aside from the earlier bad Nad's experience, I had new fears. What if my vulva looked weird? What if the professional waxer had to lift my stomach or thighs to get to the hair? What if it smelled odd because I was so nervous I just sweated everywhere? I wasn't sure I was ready to show my private parts to a woman who was probably much younger than me, and make excuses for how things looked down there. A reality I only recently came face-to-face with, myself.

I was thirty the first time I really looked at my vagina. I knew it was there, I'd felt it a bunch, others had seen it, three kids had come out of it, so yeah, it's been around. But

I'd never actually gotten a mirror and looked at things my-self. Looking down at it is not an option, not with big boobs or a stomach.

I once tried to use my phone to take a picture of it, but the angle was wrong and I couldn't find an agreeable filter. I even tried setting my phone on the floor between my legs, squatting down and taking video, but it ended up looking like the Lorax was attempting to give my iPhone CPR.

I eventually got Andy involved and asked him to really quickly take a flattering picture of my pubic hair, which he did with absolutely no questions asked. Apparently after eleven years of marriage, nothing I say surprises him.

Things looked okay; normal, really. Nothing was hang-ing out, bumpy, or discolored. It didn't look like they do in pornos, because those women have their labia lips removed, but it definitely looked young. Not underage young, but a solid twenty-seven at the most.

As I moved forward with my decision to wax, I began ca-sually talking to friends who mentioned having had it done, but there's no classy way to ask, "So hey, did they have to lift your fat up, or was the table inclined so everything just kinda rolled back on its own?"

Chubby-girl foreskin, it's a thing.

Eventually I figured the only way I was going to get all the answers I needed was to just go get waxed. It took me a bit to find someone who did full Brazilian waxes, and not just bikini waxes. The difference being that a Brazilian wax removes all of the hair, and a bikini wax simply removes the sides so that it doesn't creep out of your bathing-suit bottoms. If I was getting my pubic hair pulled off, I was doing the whole thing.

My waxer's name was Rachel, and she had great eyebrows, which is something you notice when you are trying not to look someone directly in the eye. She gave me a wet wipe to quickly preclean my pubic area and a tiny paper thong to put on before climbing on the table.

She gave me privacy while I took my pants off, and from the second I put the paper underwear on, it was apparent I had overshot the hair-growth rule. They told me on the phone that I needed at least a quarter of an inch of hair for the wax to properly catch and pull the hair out. I easily had a member of the cast of *Duck Dynasty* between my legs. So much so that Rachel had to trim my hair, with scissors, before she could even begin to wax.

From the very start, it was ungodly painful. The top was the absolute worst, and there was nothing to be done. I just lay there as she ripped my hair out from the root, trying not to scream so loud it would upset the hot-stone-massage people down the hall.

Once she made her way down to the lip and inner lip area, the pain decreased by at least half. It went from wiping-a-hot-curling-iron-all-over-your-face painful to simply stepping-on-a-mousetrap-with-your-labia painful. Totally doable.

Rachel worked really quickly, and just when I thought she was done, she asked me to get on my knees and lean in to her so she could wax my anus. Which is a thing that

Google did not tell me was going to happen, and I had not prepared for. Surprisingly, waxing your butt is completely painless, which was a welcome perk to having to pull my cheeks apart for a woman I'd just met.

The entire process took maybe ten minutes, and she finished off the wax by tweezing a few stray hairs and then left the room for me to re-dress. I got off the table and immediately looked at the trash can where she'd been tossing the used strips of cloth; it looked like an Ewok had died in there.

As I slid up my pants, it was clear that I had an unprecedented amount of room in the crotch, and when I got into my car, I had to adjust my rearview mirror, as I was sitting a good two to three inches shorter.

I know that being completely hairless weirds some people out, and makes them feel childlike. I agree: it *is* a pretty icky thing to think about. But I actually loved being waxed smooth, and it made things so much cleaner and easier, especially when I was on my period.

It was like living with a Sphynx cat. I could not stop touching it, and I wanted to show it to all my friends. Strangely, everyone gets weird when you pull your pants down in a Chili's. Go figure.

Pubic hair or no pubic hair is a personal choice, and there is no wrong answer. And truth be told, my preference ebbs and flows, both because I'm lazy and terrible at scheduling appointments, and because sometimes I just really dig having a bush.

If you are interested in waxing but nervous, I want to try

to calm some of your fears. First, you are not too fat to get a Brazilian, and nobody cares what your vagina looks like. Trust me, waxers are professionals who have seen all sorts of women and all sorts of vaginas, and unless there's a baby leg hanging out, yours is not the weirdest they've ever seen.

Also, don't worry about the smell. I mean, worry about the smell if it's suspicious and you need a doctor or something, but we all have scents, and before you get your wax, you'll most likely have to wipe yourself down with cleansing wipes or powder, then put on paper underwear, and everything is kosher. Trust me.

As for having to move your squishy parts around to reach hair, that will probably happen. But I want to assure you that my waxing was done in the most nonchalant and "no big deal" way possible. I actually tried to intervene a lot my first time, pushing my inner-thigh fat down and stretching my whole body out straight to try to make my vagina look less chubby. Rachel had to bat my hands away and tell me to stop. Waxers know what positions work best to reach the hair, they know which positions minimize pain, and they know that they are waxing human people. As such, they fully expect that those people come with things like tummies and thighs, or in my case, fat vaginas.

Remember that a Brazilian wax means they wax everything, including your butt . . . because apparently there's still ape hair there. WTF evolution? I know you think it will be embarrassing, especially if, say, you have a really, really cute post-kid hemorrhoid there or something, but it's not.

And it's also the least painful area they wax, so you might as well enjoy it.

Lastly, be prepared for effects that extend beyond suddenly needing smaller-size underwear and obsessively petting yourself. Peeing was weird at first. I don't know why, but I went from having a normal stream of pee to what can only be described as the sprayer thing attached to your sink that has, like, one wonky-clogged spray hole that makes it go all weird. It's cool now, but I needed goggles for a while until I got things under control.

All in all, my waxer, Rachel, is one of the most women-positive people I know, which makes sense: she's on the front line of an intimate battle.

And hey, always tip your waxer nicely. There are people you need to keep happy in life, and the person who willingly waxes your butthole is one of them.

Women need to feel insecure about doing something for themselves like they need another hole in the head.

YOU HAVE MY PERMISSION TO HATE YOURSELF

Listen, it's totally cool if you hate your body today. I just want to take that pressure off you right from the start. I'd also like to say, "Hey, me too!"

I'm in that weird time before my period starts when I plan to eat everything and wear nothing that deals with buttons, constriction, or a waist of any kind. I have no immediate plans to entertain guests, I'm avoiding the mirror and selfie camera, and I cringe when my husband or children touch my body.

I used to feel very ashamed about feeling this way. Hating yourself is a very isolating situation, so much so that it tricks you into thinking you're the only one to ever have these thoughts of disgust about yourself. You are not.

Some could argue that not liking yourself is one of the easiest things you can do, and that loving your body is actually very hard. Based on zero scientific evidence beyond knowing lots of women and collectively hating our bodies at various points in our lives, I'm here to tell you that it is probably true.

DISCLAIMER: Yes, it's hard to see my body as a failure sometimes. It feels selfish and wrong. Here I am, waking up every morning, walking around without any known diseases. I'm running and jumping and playing with my kids, ultra-aware that what I'm doing—this heart-beating, lung-expanding, intestines-doing-whatever-the-hell-they-do thing—is very much a privilege.

I'm privileged to have organs that do what they are supposed to do. I'm privileged to have legs that walk and eyes that see, and not be in a hospital somewhere, or worse, gone. Those are privileges.

How do I justify spending so many moments of extreme privilege hating this magnificent machine that I walk around in? I have a body that performs all these complicated scientific miracles that I could never possibly understand, and yet I never say thank you. I never say "how glorious" or "thank God." I never high-five myself and think, *Hey, good job on that digestion earlier!*

Instead, I take it completely for granted and go on

to bitch and complain the whole time. My brain has evolved into a snarky Monday-morning quarterback.

"Hey, congratulations on receiving that humanitarian award last night, but maybe you could have eaten less bread at the table."

"I like your new driver's-license photo, the shadow from your forehead really hides your double chin."

Listen, it's a miracle that you are alive today. Many, many people do not get that privilege. You can change lots of things in this life, but one thing you can't change is the fact that you can never get back time. There are no do-overs. No chances to join in and live more when instead you sat out, and all those other feel-good greeting-card sayings. This is it.

All that being said, what you are feeling about yourself right now is fine and normal and allowed. Because I say so.

Some of the hardest conversations I've had about my hiccups in self-love were with my husband. And you could apply this level of hardness to almost anyone in your life. Your significant other, your mom, your best friend . . . realizing you are okay with not loving yourself every day is one thing, convincing others it's okay is an entirely different monster.

"What are you looking for?" Andy asked, leaning against the door of my walk-in closet.

"My black leggings," I answered, not looking up as I dug through a pile of black clothing on the floor.

"There's literally a whole stack on this shelf, just grab a pair so we can go." He sighed.

The tears that had been welling up in my eyes had finally reached capacity, and were spilling down my cheeks.

"Those leggings don't fit me right," I explained. "I want the ones that cover my tummy all the way and aren't worn thin in the thigh."

To the untrained eye, those leggings were no different from the leggings folded and piled next to me. They were a spandex needle in the haystack, but my self-esteem hinged on them.

"Just go without me and let me stay home," I cried.

Many of my interactions with my closet went just like this. Own five hundred things, wear only ten. When I'm not feeling my body, that list shrinks to three. But what do you say to someone to convince them that this whole hating-your-body, nothing-to-wear, everything-is-horrible thing is not only valid, but totally allowed? Here are some helpful talking points.

1. First of all, you just have to let me hate my body. Let me have my complaining and moaning, and let me just sit in it, all day long. Don't try to pacify me with "if you could only see what I see's" or "but you're beautiful's," just let me tell you what I hate

and how much I hate it. I have to carry this struggle around every minute of every day in my head. When I order food, when I catch my reflection while I wash my hands in the bathroom sink, when I'm in my car and I look down at a red light and notice my thighs squishing together. Every single second of every day is directly affected by how I feel about my weight. It's suffocating and exhausting, and sharing the burden of it with you is a welcome relief. So listen to me, don't interrupt or shake your head, listen and nod, and when I'm done, resist the urge to shower me with every ounce of beauty you see in me, and instead ask, "How can I help?"

2. Spoiler alert: You can't actually help. Be prepared to not be able to fix this shit at all. I held on to teeny-tiny jeans from high school in my closet for fourteen years, until I finally threw them away a few months ago. They were an entire person smaller than my current size, but I couldn't let go of that gut-level need to maintain the hope that I would one day fit into the stupid pants again, thus making me a better woman. Fourteen years, dude. It was adorable that my husband thought he could in some way

override the longest relationship I'd ever had with doses of unconditional love and commitment. There is no duct-tape fix for a woman hating her body.

3. The Julia Roberts *Pretty Woman* Hooker in a Boutique moment. Seriously, every woman knows what this is, and every woman needs it. After you've been shut down and rejected by aloof teens staffing mall clothing stores, there is relief in walking into a safe place, crumbled up hundred-dollar bills in your hands, and having someone genuinely help you find something you feel beautiful in.

It took Andy demanding that I take off work to go shopping for a whole day with the caveat that I could only purchase clothes for myself. He didn't have to give me permission because he's the head of the household and controls the money like in an episode of *Mad Men*. He had to give me permission because I was so not kind and encouraging to myself; my coping mechanism was to ignore my personal needs altogether; after all, as women, we often do for ourselves last. What can I say, we're a selfless breed, you're welcome, all men.

Having something to wear is an important part of self-esteem. When you want to leave the house and you're still in the bedroom distraught and sobbing that you have nothing to wear, what that really means is that you have nothing to wear that makes you feel at all worthy to be seen or loved in public. Can you imagine feeling so ashamed of your body that you won't leave the house? It's a real thing. Having pieces that genuinely fit and flatter your current shape is a game changer.

4. Help me take responsibility for myself. At the end of the day, this is on me. I have to be the one strong enough to scream "ENOUGH!" to society with its obnoxious marketing and unrealistic beauty standards, because they aren't going to change anytime soon. What will change is the way I let those standards affect me. While you can't step in and fix my self-esteem issues, you can be a really great model of strength and advocacy I can learn from, and eventually apply to my own body issues.

Is my overbearing mom commenting on every forkful of food I bring to my lips? Speak up and defend me until I'm ready to tell my mom to shut the hell up, myself. Note: I'm all for feminism, but defending my honor is one of my biggest turn-ons.

Is your friend making fun of fat chicks while watching the football game in your living room? Shut it down until I get the tits to stand up and remind him how damn sexy all women are, regardless of size.

Strength and confidence are contagious. I like to use the clichéd analogy of climbing Everest. I will never reach the peak, but over time, I'll stumble less and climb to higher base camps. Sometimes the best you can do is be my Sherpa; offering guidance when asked, repeating uplifting feminist Emma Watson quotes in times of need, and helping me take really cool selfies.

5. Realize that body hate is a shapeshifter. Some days it comes as finicky hair or a run in our tights; other days as the tsunami of tears in our car outside of work. Both are consuming, and like an iceberg, you might only see the tip, so it's easy to think, *Just get over it.* But what you don't see is what's lurking underneath the water; a mountain of anxiety and self-doubt. Treat both with equal amounts of understanding and seriousness, because to us, they're both the same amount of day-ruining horribleness.

On the flip side of all of this, it's okay to be excited about your body. Heck, I highly encourage it, every chance you get.

For some reason, women are made to feel bad for

both loving and hating their bodies. That means being a woman is a losing battle. If we feel bad about our bodies, we're failures; if we feel good about them, we're arrogant and conceited. Neither of these is true.

It's okay to walk out of the fitting room and take a look in the big general-population mirror, not because you want a better look at the fit of what you're trying on, but because you know you look fly as hell. You peacock your way all around that dressing room aisle runway, and if I sense you doing it, I'll open up my door and I'll applaud you. You'll recognize me as the girl with the pale legs trying on bathing suits with ankle socks.

This is also why I love seeing my social media channels congested with selfies. I'd rather see constant documented moments of life than worry that my friends don't feel important enough to be captured and shared. I don't even care if you filter the photo beyond recognition and you live your selfie life in a Barbara Walters soft-focus haze; do what makes you feel confident, and eventually one day you'll decide to show up in my feed sans Clarendon.

These love/hate feelings for your body are not mutually exclusive and can coexist from day to day—hell, from hour to hour, if you so choose. You could feel insecurity at 10 A.M. and like Ashley Graham by dinner, and that's fine.

So, while I'm giving you permission to have the bad days, know that the goal is that they come with a time limit. Wallow in those moments of frustration and disesteem, soak in every drop, and take advantage of sitting that day out. I mean, really take advantage of it; eat what makes you happy, cry because it feels good, sit pantless in the tub because it makes you feel small, live the life of self-loathing.

Once you've done all of that, take a shower and start over knowing that 90 percent of the people out to judge you are inside your own head. Nobody else cares, and I'm not saying that to be mean, I'm saying it because we're all just as busy lumbering about our lives with our own internal monologues of how much we suck. Body shame is not special and it's not unique. Everyone is just trying to feel better about themselves, and nobody really knows how. Including me. But I have a few ideas.

First, you can't hang liking yourself on some goal you hope to someday reach. Whether it's weight loss or fitting into an outfit, you can't withhold happiness as punishment. You know who does that? Disney villains. And the last thing you want is to be the bad guy in your own story. The only thing it will result in is years and years of you sitting on the sidelines being angry with yourself. And that angry face you make gives you wrinkles.

Next, you need to realize you don't owe anyone shit. Your body is yours, and only you get to decide how you feel about it today. Personally, I'm tired of explaining to people that I am healthy so they allow me to like myself. And I'm tired of hiding my insecurities because I'm afraid this will only confirm what people might be judging me for. Whether or not you are healthy, have lost weight, have an invisible disorder or disability, or went through something traumatic . . . people aren't entitled to your story, but they are required to be kind to you. You need to stop giving them parts of you in response to their judgment. Knowing you is a gift, and we don't give gifts to mean people anymore.

Know that not everyone deserves you. I know that as a fat woman, I have spent a lot of time feeling so unwanted or overlooked, and so desperate for attention or to be seen. And it was that desperation that blinded me to the crappy people around me: friends who made snarky remarks, family members who said mean things, men and women who used me because they saw my kindness and longing for love as weakness.

I am worth being selective about who I let into my life, and so are you. What you weigh in no way equates to how people are allowed to treat you.

Stop treating yourself like the unwanted person you assume you are. No one deserves to be treated badly, and one of the best ways to combat that is to show people how they should be treating you. Model it for them to take the work out of it because heaven knows people are lazy. Empathy and humanity are harder to feel than quick judgment and disgust. Confidence (even the shaky kind), sexiness, value, happiness . . . people can smell it and it's contagious. I wear my confidence like one of those creepy cats in heat with their asses in the air. It's obnoxious and forward, but it shows people there is only one way to treat me . . . awesome.

Show yourself kindness and happiness, even when it feels fake. While you are busy demanding it from everyone else, make yourself accountable as well. Body image is a lifelong journey, so enjoy it and don't save all the fun and rewards for the end, because then you'll never get there. Miserable journeys are the worst, like driving a thousand miles from Ohio to Florida. I do it twice a year, and if I didn't stop on the way for fried pies, Popeye's chicken, and fresh orange juice, I'd never get there. I'd just stop my car and lie on the road until someone moved me or ran me over. Stop lying on the road and enjoy yourself.

Buy yourself clothes that fit. They may not be the size you think you should be, but who cares? I'll tell you who doesn't care: everyone you know.

Get your hair cut and practice good hygiene. Listen, I don't care if you shave, but wash your body and take care of your skin. It's way easier to convince yourself that you are a good person who deserves to be treated well when you don't smell like a Garbage Pail Kid.

Also have sex, with someone or yourself, I don't care, just do it. Orgasms are deserved, not bones tossed at you by shallow people. Go on adventures. It's scary out there, I know. People are mean and the world isn't always accommodating to all sizes of people, but that is no excuse to lose any more time to the liars in your head. Have your bad days, and then bounce back in time to live your life laughing with friends in bars and exploring foreign countries and screaming your head off at theme parks and pools. It's what humans do, and that is exactly what you are. Human.

And there's your pep talk. I hope this book goes on to help you feel, at best, empowered, and at worst, normal. Because when you spend a good portion of your day feeling inconsequential and unworthy of love and respect, normal is a pretty amazing thing to be.

CHAPTER 8

On This Episode of Jeans Hoarders

"Here's the thing," I explain. "I could keep coming to therapy every week, or you could just come look in my jeans closet and fix my entire life."

Tom, my mustache-fidgeting therapist of six years, stares silently at me from his green plaid armchair. We've been seeing each other in a doctor-patient capacity to treat my generalized anxiety disorder.

To the average person, his office looks old and decidedly dated. Dark green papered walls, plaid furniture, faded framed photos, and a collection of vintage typewriters on the shelves behind his mahogany desk. However, fully aware that he rode his bike to work this morning and is likely hiding a jar of home-brewed kombucha somewhere in his desk, I know otherwise. Tom is eccentric on purpose. What's a stronger word than "hipster"? That word is "Tom."

"My parents are hoarders, I'm the antihoarder!" I exclaim, exasperated at his nonverbal judgment.

I have had this conversation with him close to one hundred and seventy-two times.

Even now, I can't go to visit my parents without secretly purging piles of knickknacks and junk from their counters and tossing them into the trash. When I was growing up, it was boxes of archaic technology: VHS tapes, VCR cleaning tools, laminating supplies, and Rolodexes of customers left behind from their turbulent years owning a video rental store.

In terms of hoarding, it could be worse, like garbage or cats. All of my parents' junk is clean, just overpowering in its mass; every usable space in their house was covered in boxes or stacks of paper.

As a result, I keep nothing. If papers accumulate on Andy and my kitchen counters or dressers, I toss them in panic, leaving Andy to ask things like, "Where's that check that was on the counter," or "Why are they shutting our water off, did they send a bill?"

"Right, except for jeans," Tom counters, shifting in his chair and adjusting his brown suspenders.

"I don't 'air-quote' hoard 'air-quote' jeans, Tom."

I feel the need to explain here that Tom is not my therapist's first name; rather it's a nickname he offered for his extra-long Greek surname that he must have gotten tired of me mispronouncing. I was raised to always call people by their formal titles, but didn't even realize my parents had names and identities outside of "mom" and "dad" until much later than normal. It was like finding out that Bob Saget wasn't actually all-American dad Danny Tanner, but, rather, this tall guy who told dirty dick jokes in seedy comedy clubs.

"How many pairs do you own?" Tom asks.

"Who really knows?" I sigh, leaning back into the couch and covering my tummy with the jacket I'd brought along, not because it was cold that day, but because I was feeling self-conscious about my arms.

"Where do you keep them all?" Tom asks.

"The denim closet."

"The Gap has a denim closet, Brittany; normal people don't have denim closets."

When Candy Spelling dedicated a whole room to wrapping paper, it was a magazine-worthy design innovation, but when I create a denim closet, it's on the same level as Jeffrey Dahmer storing human arms in his freezer.

Okay, truth time. I own fifty-eight pairs of jeans; of those fifty-eight pairs, I cycle through the same three pairs until I eventually wear the inner thighs thin, mourn them as they lie in state on the floor of my closet, and eventually throw them away in the kitchen garbage can, prompting Andy to ask me, "Hey, did you mean to throw these jeans in here?" a million times, endlessly throwing salt into my wound.

"You should really go through that closet" is a phrase

that I often hear. I hear it from Tom and Andy, and I hear it from my mom, who, after being suddenly laid off from the medical office she helped run for almost two decades, came to run Andy and my home so I could get some damn work done. Originally, she was just supposed to watch the kids, and intervene so I wasn't opening Go-Gurt tubes every five minutes when I was trying to write, but her responsibilities evolved to total house care and management after she, ironically, got tired of me not keeping it tidy enough.

"One day you're going to find my body under two hundred pounds of denim, Brittany." What a silly complaint.

I don't want to sound trite here, but mine is not just an obnoxious closet filled with denim. It's a chamber of possibility. When I stand inside it, it's like that scene when Willy Wonka (the Gene Wilder version, not the creepy Johnny Depp one) first introduces the golden ticket holders to his edible magic factory.

"Come with me, and you'll be in a world of pure imagination . . ."

Within those shelves, you'll find my favorite jeans from junior high school, the American Eagle flare. These jeans are a size 14 and were produced before jeans were filled with stretch and spandex, which probably means that they are now the equivalent of a child's 5T. Jeans without stretch are almost impossible to find these days, making my American Eagle flares Smithsonian-worthy.

I tried to put them on once and they only got to the middle part of my shins, where the grocery cart hits if you're not paying attention and looking up drink recipes on your phone while you shop. I will never be able to wear these jeans again, and yet I will never get rid of them.

Tom was right. I may not hoard cats or sports memorabilia, but I hoard emotions, dreams, and memories, and I store them in jeans that don't fit me anymore. If I was Voldemort, I'd turn my jean overalls from high school into a horcrux.

Why yes, I do have jeans in that closet ranging from sizes 14 to 22, and no, it has nothing to do with my inability to understand basic measurement, and everything to do with the fact that I'm a woman, and brands lack the courtesy to give you an accurate standard of sizing. At Old Navy, I wear a size 14. At American Eagle, I'm now a 16. Gap requires I wear an 18. At Torrid, I'm a 20. And at Anthropologie, I'm whatever size Oliver Twist was as he longingly pressed his little orphan face against the window from the sidewalk because nothing in that store fit him or me.

I know that if I go jeans shopping for my husband, he's a size 32x32. Everywhere, he's a size 32x32. He doesn't even have to try anything on, he just walks up to a pile of pants, grabs a pair, and then pays for them. He even takes the tags off them before trying them on once he gets home; that is the level of fit confidence we are talking about here, guys. Thanks to brands playing loosey-goosey only with women's sizing, my husband lives a life I will never know.

By this same moronic sizing phenomenon, I also have identical pairs of jeans in my closet in a variety of sizes. This is called bracketing, and it's commonly done when you are ordering clothes online and unsure of your size, which is often the case for plus-size women, because we generally don't really get to shop in brick-and-mortar stores like everyone else. Instead we are stuck ordering a haul online, and returning whatever doesn't work. Except I don't return the jeans, not because I'm lazy (which I am), but because I like having access to my favorite style of jeans no matter what my body is shaped like that day. Spoiler alert: It's often guinea-pig shaped.

"Anything you want to, do it . . ."

Everyone has a dream outfit. A lot of times it's a fancy dress or a sexy bathing suit, but for me, it's basically every candid photo ever taken of a British royal: button-up shirt, skinny jeans, and tall riding boots. I want to look like I just finished my bird-hunting trip and now I have to go back to my country home to cuddle my menagerie of dogs and text with J. K. Rowling.

The key to this entire outfit is the skinny jeans. Tall boots with any other type of pant simply do not work. No matter how you fold them, you still walk around looking like Napoleon and not like you just spent a chilly morning picking out fresh French bread at the farmers' market while sipping coffee from an earth-friendly thermos made from all the recycled plastic bottles that were otherwise murdering dolphins and polar bears.

The biggest obstacle to my achieving this outfit goal, aside from the button-up shirt, which is a legitimate big-boobed hate crime across the board, is overcoming the term "skinny jeans." I've never been skinny anything, and since all my weight is in my thighs, skinny jeans have always terrified me. How could jeans that cling to my body be flattering and/or fit me?

It turns out that buying a great pair of dark wash skinny jeans makes even the chubbiest of legs, like mine, look longer and leaner by getting rid of all that extra fabric flopping around and giving you a nice straight line. Skinny jeans are a fat girl's best friend. In fact, they're everyone's best friend. Of the fifty-eight pairs of denim in my closet, I'd say roughly two dozen fall into this category.

Then there are the high-rise varieties stuffed in there. I used to equate a high rise with being old and out of style. Like the people who were four years ahead of you in high school that at one time you thought were the epitome of badass. But then you run into them at a bar somewhere ten years later and they're still wearing those classic-cut light wash jeans, a braided brown belt, and a faded hypercolor T-shirt with DAMN GINA! across the front. They don't look cool anymore; they look like losers. Or your parents.

And you think, *How does this happen? Do they not have access to the Internet? Or* People *magazine?*

The answer is that they do . . . they're just further along in the process than you! They've already realized that low-rise jeans are for male country stars or regular people with well-maintained pubic hair who own small-size underwear and don't mind pulling their pants up every time they sit down, stand up, or bend over. Low-rise jeans don't even have real pockets—just tiny slits that you can fit one, *maybe two,* Starbursts in. That's blasphemy as far as I'm concerned.

The last time I wore low-rise jeans was to my friend Laura's bachelorette party, and all night long, in every single bar, I had to stand. Sitting on a barstool meant everyone behind me was going to see my love handles, tramp stamp, and butt crack. These are three sexy details of my body I typically reserve for my super-lucky husband. All night long, I perched in my really uncomfortable heels. No jeans are worth that. But, you know, that pair is still stuffed in that closet, too.

So high-rise jeans are now my happy place, showcasing everything I love about my body: my hips and my thigh curves. These are the parts of me that my husband likes to grab on to when he kisses me in the kitchen, the parts of me that sway when I walk, and that look good hidden and uncovered.

I read an article once that listed various female trends that men hated; among the most mentioned were fake nails, heavy makeup, and high-waisted jeans because they looked like "mom jeans." First of all, are we also making a list for men? Because I'd like to have a conversation about the open-sided tank tops, Oakley sunglasses, and cargo shorts, 'kay?

Second, suspending the reality that men have absolutely any say in what we wear, what's wrong with mom jeans? Mom jeans mean two things: (1) Somewhere along the line, someone is getting laid. And (2) In the words of Amy Poehler and Tina Fey, bitches get shit done, and we're far too busy running the world to pull our pants back up every ten minutes. Hence, after the skinny jeans, these are the most popular variety featured in my denim chamber of secrets.

Button fly, zipper, elastic waist, maternity panel, skinny, flair, bootleg, all of these many varieties can be found in my denim closet. I see the pros and cons of all of them (except for the bootlegs. Those just look bad on me. My thighs are too thick for the cut to look right. They just look like baggy pants).

I generally prefer an elastic waist to a zipper/button combo as the latter tends to handicap my ability to function at my desired level of food consumption. When I am on my period, I would love to eat a size 22 amount of french fries, but the dictatorship of society's zipper and button constraints only allow me a size 6 portion.

American Eagle recently started releasing button-fly jeans again, like in the nineties. Who exactly is the demographic for these pants? Certainly not people who have to use the bathroom in a hurry, so I hope they come with a catheter. I guess that's why American Eagle's primary shopper is a fifteen-year-old girl who hasn't pushed a watermelon out of her vagina yet. Hopefully.

Then there are the jeggings. Jeggings are the sister pant to skinny jeans, as in the sister who always asks you for money and gets tattoos she regrets. They are what would happen if your comfy period underwear and a full-body pair of Spanx had a baby, which sounds amazing, and it is, as long as the fabric is thick enough. If the jegging denim is thin, they show all of my thigh dimples and creases.

They are great for large holiday meals, or riding the mechanical bulls at the bar your friends drag you to because they think the bartender is interested in them. I make all my best worst decisions wearing jeggings.

And last but not least are the maternity jeans I keep among all the other types of denim. Why do I keep them, you ask, when my youngest is eight years old? Because I made the decision that it is still okay to wear them once in a while. And what's not to like about this decision? You can eat forever in these pants, they are really easy to slip off when you are having sex on the basement steps while your kids watch *Dora the Explorer,* and they virtually eradicate the muffin top.

My maternity jeans have become a Thanksgiving and Christmas tradition, something Andy originally scoffed at until he realized it meant I wouldn't be unbuttoning my pants at his grandmother's table anymore.

There is nothing lazy about comfort, and if stretchy maternity jeans make you happy, you should wear them. Maybe Martin Shkreli would have been a better person if his pants were elastic.

I doubt it.

There was a time in my life when I gave up jeans altogether. I had gotten to a point where I was so uncomfortable in restrictive clothing that I stopped buying jeans and just lived in leggings seven days a week.

My return to denim was a sign of confidence and body love. I finally felt comfortable leaving the house. I finally felt comfortable spending money on myself. I finally felt comfortable wearing real pants. So what if they didn't always have zippers?

But even now it can be a defeating process. The original title of this book was *Drinking in My Closet,* because I still spend a lot of my time doing just that. I have the type of body that has trouble shopping off the rack, that will have a fitting room success rate in the low teens, and that gets easily frustrated when I'm trying on piles of online orders and none of them are fitting me like they did on the fake plus-size model on the website.

And jeans are the biggest offender. Next is hats, I have a seriously large head. Someone make me stop ordering them, they never fit. But I keep trying. And I always will.

So maybe I am a denim hoarder. I'm okay with it.

CHAPTER 9

Fat and Pregnant

If I could go back in time to before I had my first baby, I would erase everything on my Babies"R"Us registry and make only one request: twenty pairs of mesh hospital underwear.

Everything else you can figure out; people had babies just fine without wipe warmers and baby jeans. Babies don't need to wear jeans. Babies don't even need pockets; they have no money or iPhones.

There is something magical in that mesh underwear. If you are not familiar, it can best be described as a boy short made of a stretchy fishnet material, and it's the first piece of clothing they put on you after you have a child.

The whole childbirth experience is very surreal. You do

nothing for yourself in the moments after except stare into the eyes of the beautiful new mushy being in your arms, totally unaware of the bustle unfolding around you. There's a doctor seated between your legs sewing up the aftermath, and a nurse next to your bed, looking up from her paperwork every few minutes to smile at your new family before returning to her notes. A second nurse buzzes about, pulling the bloodied hospital gown from your body and replacing it with a clean one, and then, as if she was caring for her own child or elderly parent, she rips the backing from a giant maxi pad, sticks it to the inside of the mesh underwear, and slides them up your legs and up around your butt, all things you can't do yourself because you're still numb from the waist down.

I was never a morning birther; all of my kids came conveniently after the hospital cafeteria and kitchen were closed. So after working a whole person down my birth canal for twenty hours on nothing but a diet of water and ice chips, I was given two prepackaged deli sandwiches from the overnight fridge, wheeled to my room, and left alone with my food and baby for the very first time.

It was only then, after I settled into the soft bed, that I peered over the head of my nursing infant to check the damage. My stomach looked much the same as it had the day before, but was now soft and still. That is actually one of the more trippy aspects of childbirth: once you have the baby, you begin to recognize their movements, and remember what they felt like from the inside.

The swelling in my ankles and feet was starting to sub-side, and feeling was returning to my calves and toes.

But my pubic area was just a mess of padding and ice packs and tape all stuffed into an adult diaper made from the mesh of an eighties tank top. At first glance, it was a car crash. But once I stood up, and waddled around the room a bit, I quickly realized I was wearing the most comfort-able underwear on the planet. This one-size-fits-all garment is flattering, perfectly soothing against your still-inflated stomach, and feels like you are wearing everything and yet nothing, all at the same time. And if that's not enough, it also holds all the gear you need to address the pain shooting out from your vagina.

How are these not sold in mainstream markets? Why are we not seeing these on the Angels clomping down a Victoria's Secret runway? Is it because we can only trick women into buying sexy underwear if it also feels like the crotch is made of a hairbrush? The market would be huge. We're talking actual see-through underwear made sexier by the fact that you can store stuff in them. Like hamster cheeks. Mesh-hamster-cheek underwear.

Shortly after the birth of my third child, our daughter, Gigi, Andy and I agreed it was time for a vasectomy. Some-thing he will be quick to tell you was "really painful, and really hard to describe it to someone who hasn't experi-enced it firsthand."

It became pretty obvious postclipping that his boxers were ill equipped to support the bags of frozen vegetables he strategically layered around his scrotum, so I selflessly dug into my hidden mesh-panty inventory and fixed him up with a bag of frozen pearl onions.

My youngest daughter is eight, and I still have eleven pairs of mesh underwear from her birth. I keep them on hand, not only for myself, but because I like to slip a pair into baby-shower gift baskets. The recipient always looks slightly confused until the moms around her realize what is in her hands and circle her, cooing and nodding their heads.

"Let us sing you the song of our people!"

Everyone tells you to grab as many free diapers, swaddling blankets, and pacifiers as you can from the baby cart they wheel into your room each day, and you should: that stuff is amazing. But as all the mothers on baby and birth forums preach, it's the panties that are the true treasure. I've even tried to find them online, but it is just one of those things that are really hard to replicate, so you have to take really good care of them.

My whole life, I've never adhered to a hand-wash- or dry-clean-only tag, in fact I've never even been inside a dry cleaner. However, despite my past neglect for general fabric-care instruction, there I was delicately hand-washing the blood out of my onetime-use, completely disposable, beloved mesh underwear, and then lining them up to dry over the shower curtain bar.

In a way, I think the mesh underwear is used to prepare you for motherhood, at least the early stages when nothing is conventionally attractive and everything is stretchy and important.

I want to cut in really quick here because while pregnancy is a really amazing experience, and we're totally going to talk more about navigating it, I want to touch on the fact that it is also an experience that is routinely ruined by gobs and gobs of assholes.

Some of them are people you know, some of them are strangers who come up to you in stores, some of them write columns in glossy magazines or on the Internet, and some of them are, *gasp*, doctors.

Obviously, I am not a doctor, and you should seek medical advice from me *never*, but I have to ask, at what point did we declare open season on women's pregnant bodies? I gained sixty pounds during my first pregnancy, turned around, got pregnant again right away, and gained twenty more pounds. That is an eighty-pound weight gain in less than a year. And let me tell you something: pregnancy is the kindest I have ever been to my body.

I had spent twelve of the twenty-four years prior to my first pregnancy taking diet pills that would land me in the hospital with tachycardia, spitefully starving myself, taking laxatives, wearing down the enamel of my teeth throwing up just so I could maintain and not gain any more weight, and mentally punishing myself after every uncontrollable binge. I've googled how to purchase a tapeworm with a level of seriousness that was both undeterred and grotesque.

But most people don't notice any of that when they see

me sitting in a restaurant pregnant and eating off the same menu they ordered from. They see me as someone being gluttonous, careless, indulgent, and using pregnancy as an excuse to "eat for two," when the honest-to-God truth is that I was sufficiently eating for one for the very first time in a very long time.

Gaining eighty pounds in order to bring two perfect little boys into this world was one of the most selfless things I've ever done, because I finally valued something more than I wanted to be skinny. And I did it all under the care of a medical professional whom I saw in a real doctor's office, because that is where sane people go to get their medical advice. They don't get it from nasty women in the yogurt aisle of the grocery store or from doctors on the Internet who pile on pregnant celebrities, or from anyone in a YouTube comment section.

I've had skinny friends who have gained weight, I've had fat friends who've lost weight, and the only "right" way to do pregnancy weight is with your doctor. Everyone else can suck it.

I know it's not for everyone, but I actually enjoyed the physical aspects of being pregnant. The mental aspect was terrifying. Nine whole months of trying to keep the baby alive, scrutinizing everything I ate (see above), mentally counting kicks, and then freaking out about the kicks. It was exhausting, and I thought it would all just be okay once the baby was finally born, so then that happened and I immediately realized babies were way easier to care for while they were still inside me. But my obstetrician only took them out, he didn't put them back in, so I was stuck with them out here.

So yeah, aside from that, I loved pregnancy.

Pregnancy addressed all the ways I'd previously been unenthused about my body. First, my stomach, which had been soft and doughy, and without definition, was suddenly rock-hard. It took putting a whole person inside me to give me abs, and I was totally okay with that.

As previously discussed, my prepregnancy boobs were long and uneventful. It's like all the fat just sat in my nipples and pulled them down like socks full of pennies; bad for foreplay, awesome for Mafia hits. Pregnancy inflated them, making them swollen and veiny, and my nipples grew darker and more sensitive. Couple this with the fact that I was always panting and out of breath, it was like I was a living sex doll.

Lastly, there was the hair. Ladies, pregnancy is a nine-month span where scales could cover your entire body, but add a head of pregnancy hair, and they'd legitimately choose you as the next Bachelorette. Men and women would fight over you. That is how amazingly full and glossy pregnancy hair is. It's like fetuses are full of biotin and Pantene.

Biologically speaking, pregnancy was really going well for me, but that is where the honeymoon ended. Pregnancy fashion was rough, but plus-size pregnancy fashion in 2006,

2007, and 2009 had just barely evolved past the giant tarp they threw over the dead bodies on *Law & Order*.

Best-case scenario, get pregnant during the cold months so you swell and sweat less. Then again, being pregnant in the summer means you get to wear less clothes and float around a pool like a martini olive.

So yeah, kinda sucks either way.

Congratulations, you're pregnant! Now get ready for exactly no one to notice, because chances are you don't look pregnant at all.

Assuming this is your first pregnancy . . . My second and third pregnancies had me looking six months pregnant by the time Andy pulled out. But for the first one, that just didn't happen, and it was really upsetting. When you find out you are pregnant—on purpose at least—looking pregnant is something you are really excited about. And as an overweight woman, I was especially excited to finally feel justified in the way my body looked.

I wasn't just fat, I was fat with a purpose!

Unfortunately I, like many like many women both thin and fat, spent the first few months of my pregnancy looking not so much with child but, rather, bloated. The kind of bloated where you think three slices of pizza is the right amount, but you get cocky and go for four anyways, and you're uncomfortable the rest of the night. It's *that* feeling all day, and it makes it incredibly hard to dress.

The good news is that during the first trimester, many of the clothes you are currently wearing will still work for you, especially if they are baggy and flow away from the stomach. My wardrobe just had to meet two basic criteria: Is it comfortable? And can I clean it easily if I throw up on it?

I spent a lot of time wearing cotton sun- and maxi-dresses, but when I had to actually wear pants, I was pretty insistent on making my normal jeans work, and I did so by using what is called the rubber-band trick. Thread a rubber band through the buttonhole of your jeans, and then pull one end of it through the other, securing it to your pants. Use that rubber band as the new "buttonhole." This trick is equally effective for both early maternity jeans and twenty-five-cent-all-you-can-eat wing night.

Once you hit the second trimester, you begin to panic, especially if you haven't "popped" yet. I promise, it's completely normal. Everyone pops on their own time, and popping may not even look the same for you as it does for other women. Depending on your body type, you may carry very low, or high near your ribs. Some women get really wide, some don't even look pregnant from the back, and some women get what is called a B-belly or double belly, which makes them look as if the pregnancy is being carried high, with the skin from a muffin top above or mother's apron below.

But regardless of where you are in the bloat-to-belly-pop transition, now is the time for maternity clothes. Stop dragging your feet on this and trust me. I tried to play it all cool. I mean, it is hard to embrace the idea that your life is changing completely and revamp your entire wardrobe at the same time. I stalled as long as I could. But by my second trimester there was no time to lose. I can't remember my bozo reasoning for putting off buying maternity jeans, probably some misguided belief that elastic pants were an admission of defeat, but I was an idiot. Trying on my first pair of maternity jeans was like taking off a pair of stilettos after a night of dancing: pure orgasmic relief.

There are quite a few options when it comes to maternity jeans, but the two most popular styles remain demi-panel and full panel. A demi-panel is a stretchy panel that runs around the top of a jean or pant, in place of working buttons and zippers, and sits below your tummy. Full-panel pants are based on the same concept, except that the panel covers the entire stomach and sits under your bra. Both of these can be a win for a girl who likes pull-on pants, but as a plus-size woman, I fell in love with the full panel.

Not only was having the panel covering my stomach and holding me in more comfortable, it also helped to create the look of a pregnant tummy by corralling all of my chubby, bloated flesh into a pretty little bump.

But, just like a lot of normal plus-size fashion, plus-size maternity fashion does this really weird thing where it skews old, basic, or gaudy. Like, bejeweled jeans, flutter-sleeve tees, and classic-cut stretchy pants. Nothing screams vibrant fertility like a good ponte slack! Just because I was knocked up didn't mean I wanted to look like a granny, especially during the second trimester when I was basically a nymphomaniac, which is actually another great argument for maternity jeans. Nothing comes off faster than elastic pants.

Finally I hit the third trimester—a trimester so uncomfortable, I put my old maternity jeans on in order to write this section. That is how uncomfortable I get just thinking about my third trimester.

I have a friend who found it infinitely helpful to remind me that during the later stages of her pregnancy, she couldn't fit into anything, so she just wore all her husband's sweatshirts over leggings, and looked adorable. Wearing Andy's sweatshirts over leggings isn't an option for nonpregnant Brittany, and it became far less of one with a baby belly.

While putting away laundry last week, I accidentally placed a pair of my jeans in Andy's closet. One morning, he put them on.

"Yikes, these aren't mine." He was standing behind me in the bathroom mirror, the jeans buttoned, and they were falling off his body the way Tom Hanks's adult clothes did when he turned back into a kid in the movie *Big*.

"Yeah, they're mine." I glared at his reflection in the mirror. "Because I'm fatter than you."

Not all women are dainty moms-to-be with bellies, and tossing on our partner's clothes isn't a privilege many of us have.

By the third trimester, everything I wore was stretchy, cool, and easy to pull down to pee every hour. Fitted tank tops (remember, rock-hard abs), maxi-dresses, and leggings were my life.

I also had several pairs of gaucho pants, but it was a different time back then, and we're not going to talk about those anymore.

There is no greater competition than the one that exists between moms and their prepregnancy jeans. For some reason, fitting into our prepregnancy jeans as soon as humanly possible wins you some sort of mom award.

"Oh my gosh, your baby is so beautiful," I gushed to the woman next to me in the waiting area of our ob-gyn.

"Thank you, I'm actually already back into my prepregnancy jeans." She smiled.

"Oh wow. That's impressive."

"Yeah, I even weigh less than I did before I got pregnant, so . . ."

And then I stabbed her. I'm kidding. It's just that we have really terrible messaging in regard to postbaby mom bodies. We watch celebrities have babies and then reemerge from their secret off-the-grid Illuminati tents slimmer than they'd been before. They sit for interviews where they're asked what they did to drop the weight, and they just smile and say breastfeeding and that they're *soooooo* busy with the baby they barely remember to eat.

Can I just say, I have never in my life been in a situation

where I've forgotten to eat? In fact, by the time I put my contacts in every morning, I've already mapped out what my next two meals will be.

Then we have magazine covers and morning shows blasting story after story about getting back to that prebaby body, and all the latest diets and trends to aid along the way. Corsets, low-carb meal planning, cardio workouts. I'm sorry, how is any of this happening when I couldn't even manage to shower myself or poop without biting down on a leather strap for the first few weeks after childbirth? Who was going to hold my baby for the three hours it was going to take to put that corset on?

Every high five we'd given ourselves as we met every milestone over the course of the last nine months goes out the window during this time. Our bodies go from actual miraculous vessels to big giant failures.

It takes nine whole months to make a baby. I don't know specifically how long eyeballs or feet take, but I know that it's a really long time of your body doing really cool stuff. Why do we expect everything to go back to normal immediately after spending months and months building an actual human? I've had a LEGO version of the Hogwarts castle partially built in the middle of my office for two years, and I gave myself less grief about that than I did about losing my pregnancy weight.

And even if you do get back to that prebaby place, it's going to take a minute, okay? It's going to take a minute for your body to revert to a place where it's not actively making fingers. Systems need to cool down. Everyone and everything just needs to relax.

As a new mom, I had no chill. Not only did I not get back into my prepregnancy jeans, but breastfeeding made me ravenously hungry, so much so that I gained more weight. So not only did none of my prepregnancy clothes fit me, but even my pregnancy clothes got tight. It was all going very badly.

Even if I had managed to drop weight, my body had changed. My stomach was deflated, but my boobs were heavy with milk, and my hips and butt had doubled in size. I blame this on the fact that I barely stood upright the first two months after giving birth. All I did was sit and nurse. And guys, my vagina got fat. I don't even know how that became a target area for weight gain, but I swear I carried all my third-pregnancy baby weight in my mons pubis. To this day I look like Hulk Hogan when I'm wearing bikini bottoms.

So, if you've had a baby or three, you are likely nodding along in agreement just about now as you relive that glory. If you haven't had any . . . well, you are welcome. Take my advice and know that you need to take a deep breath and accept the fact that going forward, some things will just be different.

You're definitely going to pee more, that's a given. And due to nursing, your nipples may morph from something fun into two numb chew toys at the ends of your boobs. My nipples are purely decorative at this point. And finally, the general shape of your body and how clothes fit will change, and that's not a bad thing, it's just new.

Once we all make peace with these realities, maybe it doesn't matter whether we get back into our prebaby clothes. Maybe we should be rewarding ourselves with new ones that celebrate the really awesome thing we just survived, fat vagina and all.

CHAPTER 10

I Dress Like a Mom Now, Apparently

For a split second, I assumed my mom style would go one of two ways: all cute boyfriend jeans, oversized sunnies, and a perfectly messy bun pushing a pram through a ritzy outdoor mall sipping iced coffee, or full-on Maria von Trapp in a dress made of curtains to coordinate with my brood's outfits as I instructed them on perfect harmony and amazing marionette action.

It turns out, I look terrible in boyfriend jeans, I can't sew, and puppets terrify me. My real postbaby style can best be described as postapocalyptic.

For starters, I think we all need to acknowledge that giving birth to a baby is a real medical event that involves months of prep and recovery. So, on top of healing and bleeding and milking and hoping your vagina regains some sense of its former self, you've also been handed a real live baby.

Andy had his impacted wisdom teeth removed and he was sent home with extra gauze and instructions not to work or be responsible for anything in the immediate future. I had another person removed from inside me via the same area I was now expected to pee out from and sit on, and they sent me home with a baby to keep alive and some Tylenol. Something does not compute. Oh, right, sexism!

How any of us managed to be dressed at all during this time in our lives is a goddamn miracle. Perhaps if I'd only decided to raise my children in a nudist colony, I might have had a higher level of self-care, especially when my only real requirement for being seen in public was wearing clothes with "no visible blood or milk on them."

When you first come home from the hospital, everything is about survival, and that looks different for both of you. There's the actual baby, who has to have specific needs met, like being fed, clean, happy, and rested. Then there is you, and the bar drops significantly with requirements such as a heart rate or a blink that's long enough to technically be considered a nap.

You realize really quickly that a happy baby is best for your mental health, so your whole day becomes consumed with chasing that happiness. You are a 24/7 diner that feeds on demand. You sing silly songs, make funny noises, and fly through diapers. Little parts of you get tucked away because it's easier. You remove your earrings, because the baby could pull them out. You stop wearing your favorite perfume, because it irritates the baby. You stop doing your hair, because you only throw it up in a bun anyways so the baby's little fingers don't get tangled in it. Your wardrobe becomes a mishmash of lingering maternity clothes, and new cheap pieces you picked up because you just wanted something easy.

This was a period during which I became very reliant on my sense of smell. I smelled the babies constantly, checking their bottoms in case they pooped, or the fat rolls under their chins to see if milk had soured there. I smelled my clothes, both on and off my body. Yes, the baby threw up on this shirt, but it blends with the print, does it smell too much for me to wear again? Have I worn this underwear already? Is this food or poop? It's food. No, it's poop; fuck.

I remember we scheduled a family and newborn shoot three months after having our first son, Jude, and the night before, I called the photographer and told her it'd only be the baby, no family photos. Andy didn't understand it, but nothing fit me or made me feel good. I was sitting on my bed surrounded by clothes that'd been torn out of the closet and tried on, and none of them made me feel pretty, my hair hadn't been done in months, and all I envisioned was this adorable family photo of Andy and Jude, and then me. People would look at that picture and think, *Yikes, that guy is way hotter than that sweaty lady holding that cute baby.*

I mean, I used to think that. Now when I see that exact photo play out on Facebook, I am like, "High five, Mom, that jerk in the clean cargo shorts better have taken you to brunch after this photo was taken!" We moms have to stick together.

I began to resent Andy during this period because when he came home from work he closed the door when he went to the bathroom, and I realized that he got to do that all day. When he had to pee, he got up from his desk and went to the bathroom by himself at his own pace, in a private room. And then he ate his lunch next to his friends, but he only spooned the food into *his* own mouth, not any of his coworkers' mouths.

I began to resent Andy when he asked me to put deodorant on the shopping list for him. I realized that I hadn't bought deodorant for myself in a really long time; my stick was still full and unused on the bathroom counter because all I did was sit on the couch all day with the baby. And I had decided that this activity did not require deodorant.

I began to resent Andy when he walked out of the bedroom in a clean pair of jeans, and when I asked him where he was going, he said nowhere. He just wanted to change into something clean.

I began to resent Andy for caring for himself.

Sometime between the doctor handing me the baby and screaming into a pillow at 4 A.M. our first night home, I made the decision that my kids should come before me, always. It didn't matter that I looked and smelled like I had crawled out of a Dumpster, as long as they were clean and dressed impeccably. I could do without so that they could look adorable.

I didn't have a winter coat until two years after I had my last child. I live in the snow belt of Ohio, and it's blistering cold. I got by, using a large green zip-up sweatshirt I'd stolen from my dad. All of my underwear was old and faded, with the elastic separating from the material. I bought liquid hem glue to fix the holes I'd worn in the inner thighs of my faded black leggings so that I could still wear them in public. It wasn't really a matter of money; it was a matter of low self-worth.

Everything I used to do for myself, the hair coloring, new clothes, and doctor visits, all felt suddenly so selfish. And it's crazy to think back to that time, treating buying pants that fit or seeing a doctor for a cough with the same level of mom shame that comes with abandoning your baby in a box at Walmart.

Not only was I putting the needs of my children above my own, I was woefully unprepared for how much being a mom stripped away from me feeling like a woman. I no longer felt like it was my goal to feel desired by anyone, it was my goal to feel like my children were well and cared for and loved. That made disappearing oh so easy.

At first there was a definite unspoken agreement that Andy and I would just buckle down and focus on keeping our heads above water. We had three babies in less than four years, and much of our day was lost to potty training, feeding, playing, rocking. I was so engulfed in all of that that I missed the exit ramp back to adult womanhood.

I just wasn't capable of being a mom *and* a woman, or a mom *and* a wife. And I went to great lengths to make the necessary excuses to prove these were indeed mutually exclusive.

I would purposely let the baby fall asleep in our bed so that Andy wouldn't try to have sex. I'd explain away my need for something by spending all my money on something for the baby, who needed it more. And I filled up all the cracks and weaknesses in my arguments with cement made from the shame and judgment I tossed toward other moms.

"Did you see that Erin and Mike went on a cruise? Who's watching their one-year-old? The burglar who's probably robbing them because they posted they were out of town on Facebook?"

"Oh, look, another Instagram selfie of Cara's new haircut. I guess that explains why she can't afford to come to baby astrology jazz yoga anymore."

"Gosh, I'd love to go on a date with you, Andy, but I'm too busy keeping our children alive."

Not only was this crazy motherhood Stockholm syndrome bad for very obvious mental health reasons, it was also very bad for my children. I was teaching them that there was a time limit to self-care, and it expired when you had kids of your own.

In case you haven't figured this out yet, there is no such time limit. Caring for and loving your kids should not come at the expense of caring for and loving yourself, even though it might feel like the right thing to do at the time.

Don't get me wrong, it's okay to take a minute to figure out this whole messy parenting thing, but I am all for you doing it in the stretchiest pants possible.

A huge part of our job as parents is being the first people in line teaching our kids how to value themselves. From childhood to adulthood, we are instilling in them the belief that they matter, that they should always be seen and heard, and that their worth is without limit.

I was giving my kids that very message from the comfort of the same clothes I'd been wearing for three days, with my matted hair in a bun, and an unexplained rash on my arm that I hadn't gone to the doctor about, right after I had walked away from my reflection in the mirror after calling myself fat in front of them no less than three times.

Then I think of my daughter, in particular, and see her growing into a strong young woman who knows her power and her voice. That woman is not hiding in the back of a photo wearing broken flip-flops and expired contacts.

I know it's hard to take time for you. It feels selfish and like you're failing as a good mom. That feeling will eventually go away, especially when you start seeing the effects of your self-worth in the way your children see you.

My kick in the ass came from an unexpected place: my children's school. Theirs, like a few others around the country, enacted a rule banning parents from wearing pajamas to school pickups and drop-offs. This was being done as a means of setting an example of professionalism for the students, and maybe to counteract the sight of first-day-of-school parents doing body shots and shotgunning pot smoke into each other's mouths in the parking lot. Although, to be fair, the joke is on the administration because I can sleep in anything, which means virtually everything I own is technically pajamas.

But this new rule meant that I now not only had to spend my mornings screaming at my kids to brush their teeth, do their hair, and put on clean clothes, I also had to do all of that for myself, too. I tried explaining to the school secretary that I wrote from home, and that my pajamas were what I actually wore to work, and she told me that I should set higher standards for myself, and that there was nothing wrong with a healthy routine of putting clean clothes on each morning.

And when I got back to my car, I sat there thinking of all the times I herded my children into the school wearing a nightgown and Ugg boots, or the time I had to run back home to grab Wyatt's forgotten history report, and appeared in the school office wearing a sweatshirt and men's boxers, or the day I forgot I had volunteered to drive for the class field trip, and had to chaperone kids to a pioneer village dressed in an adult Pikachu onesie, and I suddenly realized that this new stupid rule was enacted because of *me*.

Here I thought I was being the selfless mom driving her

kids all over and keeping it all together, when in reality, I was dressed like Cousin Eddie and I had absolutely nothing together. I don't know what rock bottom is supposed to feel like, but if an entire elementary school makes a dress code purely as an attempt to get you to wear pants, like they had a meeting about it and printed flyers and everything, I feel like maybe I had hit it.

I went home and ordered some jeggings from American Eagle, some new tank tops from Old Navy, and some flats from Target. This "mom" wardrobe was bland, nothing fancy or trendy, but it was new and clean, and the more I adjusted to getting up in the morning and putting on real clothes, and brushing my teeth, the more I remembered what it was like to feel independently human.

The next year, Andy and I ended up switching the kids' school for reasons totally unrelated to the administration making me wear pants, but effects had taken hold, and the changes began to seep into many parts of our lives. As a family, we began to leave the house, go to movies, and get family pictures taken again, with all of the actual family members. As a married couple, Andy and I were going on dates, and I was taking time out of my day to consciously stop chasing after kids, and kiss my husband because I wanted to, and because I missed that companionship and intimacy. As a woman, I was enjoying spending money on myself, buying clothes that made me feel good, and giving myself permission to check out to get a pedicure or get off by myself in the bathroom.

I was a mom raising her children to love themselves . . . and still figuring that out for myself, too.

"Push it through. Push it through!" I screamed, covering my face with my hands.

"I'm trying." Andy winced. "It's hitting something and it won't go through."

He stepped back from the chair I had dragged into the bathroom, an ice cube in one hand, a small earring in the other.

"You just need to force it through really fast," I explained.

"The hole is closed." He set the earring on the counter. "You need to go to a professional."

Clearly, Andy has never pierced his belly button with a safety pin and an ice cube on the floor of his bedroom while watching *TRL*.

It had been eleven years since I had worn earrings. In the last photo I have of me wearing them, I am sitting on a swing in the park with tiny Jude laughing on my lap. Shortly after the photo was taken, his chubby hand lurched for the dangling bronze bohemian earrings, and my mom scooped him up and playfully scolded him before looking at me and telling me that my days of earrings were over.

"You're a mom now. No more fun stuff." She shrugged.

I gave in. Then.

I pierced my nose when I turned twenty-two, and the

second night I had it, the tiny diamond stud got caught on the sleeve of Andy's sweatshirt as he reached across me in bed. He pulled it clean out, blood and clear pus leaking out of the hole as I screamed in pain. I tried to put the diamond back in, but the nose ring was shaped like a corkscrew— ironically, to keep it comfortable and from coming out—so twisting it back into the now-larger and seeping hole was impossible.

I went to the piercing shop to get the nose piercing re-done the next afternoon, and it was so painful as the piercer tried to screw the earring back in that I threw up down the front of me, asked him to stop, and decided to let the hole heal. It took a week.

But were these holes really closed? I could still see them on the front and back of my ear, and every so often when I was being particularly gross and obsessive about picking at my face in the magnifying mirror, I'd squeeze them and weird white stuff would come out. That's never a good sign, right?

My self-care routine fell into place quickly. Almost like muscle memory, one positive step forward begat another. I started getting my hair touched up every month. The oc-casional pedicure turned into a regular thing. I fell in love with shopping again, of trying new styles and clothes. I was dressing a foreign body, and instead of dreading the pro-cess, I began to embrace it and share it with the online com-munity I created through my blog.

But these earrings . . . they were the final piece. The last reclamation of the womanhood that I'd surrendered during the early days of motherhood. And the only thing that stood in the way of it was a tiny piece of skin?

I pushed the earring through my ear as hard as I could. It stung and immediately burned, but it was in.

The old hole was still there, after all.

CHAPTER 11

I Would Like to Dedicate a Moment of Silence for My Thighs

"You have the thighs of a sprinter," my dad called out as I pushed to catch up.

When I was a little girl my father would head out twice a week after dinner to run the outdoor track at his old high school. He often bounced between manic episodes of exercise and near anorexia, before long and tedious lapses of housebound depression, and lately we'd been on a manic trend.

I was eight and tagged along on his runs, desperate to soak up every ounce of him, even if it meant he would be disappointed in what I ate. I missed him so much when he'd disappear into his depression, and while neither version of him was real anymore, I preferred the one that sat at our dinner table with us and let me sing Jim Croce songs with him in his truck.

I spent my time at the track walking the benches of the stadium and acting out Paula Abdul music videos, but every once in a while joining him in running his laps. I struggled to keep up, but he assured me I had an innate sense of pace.

"Your legs are made to run." He nodded as he downed his water back at the truck and I struggled to pull my ridden-up shorts back down between my legs.

Four years later, I signed up for track and was placed on shot put. "It's where we put the sturdy girls," the coach assured me. She never even asked to see me run.

My thighs are underestimated.

I was called Thunder Thighs in the seventh grade at Centennial Quarry by a boy named David. Thunder Thighs is a ridiculous insult. As if having thighs as loud and as powerful as thunder was a bad thing—hell, that basically makes me an X-Man. But when you're a young girl, difference, even the powerful kind, is spat back at you like shame.

It was my first time at a quarry. I've always had an intense fear of them ever since I asked my mom how deep they were, and she said they were endless.

"You can never tell when you're at their deepest point," she explained. "And beneath you it's all jagged rocks, darkness, and sunken machinery."

I was with my friends Lauren and Abby, and we were meeting the three boys we'd met at the fair the week before. We had been walking around the pits before the start of the demolition derby, ogling the cars before they entered the ring to get smashed apart. Early September in Ohio is always stifling hot, and the fairgrounds were sweaty and humid. The pits reeked of gasoline fumes and oil. We grabbed cotton candy and made our way up to the grandstand to watch the leveling and were joined shortly after by two filthy, grease-covered boys who were looking for seats to watch how the car they'd been working on would do.

There was flirting and small talk, and before they left to join their friend in his eliminated car, the boy with the dusty brown hair turned around, ripped a chunk of Lauren's blue cotton candy from its stick, and popped it in his mouth.

"We're going to the quarry tomorrow." He smirked, walking backward down the row of bleachers. "Meet us there?"

I had no intention of getting into the water. I was wearing a neon-pink bikini borrowed from Abby's single and dating mother, and it barely fit. The top was heavily padded and tight around my ribs, and the bottom was cut so high that the roll of my lower stomach sat exposed in the leg opening. I covered it with a pair of linen drawstring shorts and planned to lie on my stomach in the sand and read magazines on the beach.

"Let's jump off the platform!" Abby squealed.

That was a hard no for me, but she begged and begged, and finally, when the boys got up to buy food at the concession stand, I took the chance to slip out of my shorts and run to the line forming below, without giving them a closer look at my body.

As I made my way up the steps and walked onto the platform alone, I was petrified. This was the highest I had ever been above an endlessly deep pool of jagged rocks and sunken machinery, and yet I was more afraid of not jumping and therefore having to walk back to my towel in the sand in front of three boys I barely knew.

I closed my eyes and jumped straight into the quarry below, shooting down so deep that the bottoms of my feet felt the cold water below the warm safety of where the sunlight hit. Panicked, I climbed back to the surface and swam to the shallow beach to catch my breath. I felt terrified and energized and alive, and that buoyant feeling carried me back to my towel, which I quickly grabbed from the ground and wrapped around my waist in front of our friends.

"Did you see that?" I asked, my chest still heaving and panting with excitement.

Lauren and Abby cheered and high-fived, and I settled back into my spot in the sand and grabbed my Coke, meeting David's eye and smiling. David had long blond hair that he kept tucked behind his ears, and wore round John Lennon glasses and cutoff denim jean shorts.

As Lauren and Abby started talking about going back to school and where their lockers were, I nodded along and watched out of the corner of my eye as David slowly huddled into his friend Jeff and whispered, "Whoa, she has thunder thighs, you can have her."

Jeff laughed and shook his head no, playfully punching his friend in the arm.

As my friends continued chatting I slowly slid my shorts on underneath my beach towel, and spent the rest of the afternoon on my stomach in the sand.

Before leaving, the boys asked us to join them later that night to see a movie, but I told them my stomach hurt and stayed home.

My thighs are unwanted.

I used to love science when it was more of an arts-and-craft project and less of a chemistry class. I was really good at painting planets and cracking open homemade geodes, anything beyond that slipped right out of my head. The only reason I wasn't failing was because I completed every extra-credit assignment available, and pestered the teacher with the flash cards I created before every test. I still didn't get many of the answers right, but he saw I was obviously trying. Honestly, I think I exhausted him, and he seriously didn't want to have to put up with me another year if I had to retake his class.

I sat in a quad of four desks. My friend Jordan sat to my right, and sitting directly across from us was a sophomore named Daniel and a senior boy named Beau. Of the four of us, Jordan was the most science-minded, carrying us through the majority of our labs and study guides, and like me, pretending not to be bothered by Daniel's incessant pestering. Daniel threw balls of paper at our chests, trying to make baskets in the necks of our shirts, and he tried, and failed, to turn words like "inertia" or "fulcrum" into innuendo.

He's the annoying guy you invite to the party out of a desire to be nice, but then he shows up an hour early and only responds to you using quotes from Jim Carrey movies while you're trying to finish setting up.

While I was sitting at my desk reading, Daniel tosses his pen at my ankle, leaving a blue streak above the platform black loafers I'd worn that day. He slides out of his seat to grab it, and very obviously tries to look up into the now eye-level black skirt I'd worn that day. I coughed and squeezed my already touching thighs even tighter.

Annoyed, he drops back into his chair.

"Your thighs are like the Berlin wall, nobody can see past them." Daniel and Beau laugh and whisper more about my legs and other body parts as my face burns. I'd been exasperated by this idiot the entire quarter, but in this moment, I was the one feeling stupid. I was angry at myself, angry that my body was (again) the problem and not the boy trying to see my panties in the middle of class.

A boy, by the way, who was so insecure about his own body that he was rumored to have sex with girls through the zipper hole of his jeans without pulling them down. I let *that* boy make me feel bad about my body.

My thighs are unwitting obstructionists.

That night, Beau taps on my dark bedroom window. He

is sleeping over at the house of his best friend, who lives across the street, but the friend fell asleep and Beau wanted to see me. We work in tandem, knowingly popping the screen out of my window, me lending a hand as he eases his way into my room.

He has been here many times before. Sometimes we kiss for hours. Sometimes I unzip his pants and go down on him while he moans into the pillow he's placed over his face. Sometimes he talks to me about his girlfriend, and how stuck he feels because his parents love her but he doesn't know if he does. We always sit with each other in the dark. I never ask why he can't see me with the lights on.

Tonight he doesn't talk to me; he only kisses me and pushes me against the wall. We both freeze and listen for a moment to make sure there is no sound coming from my parents' bedroom next door, and that no dogs are startled or made suspicious by the light thud my head made against the wall.

Beau pulls the nightgown over my head and kisses my soft stomach as he rolls my underwear down my legs. He pushes his hand inside of me so hard I begin to gasp, but he kisses me quickly and smiles into my teeth.

He moves his hand so fast and so deep, I feel something pop inside me and warm my thighs. I am as sturdy as Jell-O. He reaches his free arm around my back and lays me on the bed and kisses me for one hundred more years before crawling back out of my window.

This was his apology for the cruel way he'd spoken to me.

I quietly made my way to the bathroom, carefully shutting the adjoining door to my parents' bedroom, and I surveyed my body. My lips were pink and swollen, and as I lifted up my cotton nightgown, my legs were streaked with blood, further smeared around and sticky from the rubbing together of my thighs as I walked.

Not period blood, but from the pop I felt as if a wall inside me had been knocked down. I didn't wash it from my legs, and I grabbed a dark brown towel from the linen closet and laid it on my sheets before climbing into bed and going to sleep thinking of Beau.

My thighs do not hold grudges as long as they should.

I am not a seamstress, but I am the Betsy Ross of denim. I do most of my needlework naked, standing over the counter in my bathroom, mentally calculating how many more swishes of the thigh the now paper-thin material of the jeans can withstand.

My thighs do not know Urban Outfitters, they have never entertained 7 For All Mankind, and they do not speak the language of the thigh gap. What my thighs do know is temporary. From jeans to the soft layer of flesh that lines them, both things are rubbed away far too easily between my legs.

In the summer I wear dresses, and jack my legs onto the counter in my bathroom and lube my inner thighs with scentless deodorant, or chafing gel, or powder. A carousel of things, really, all with the purpose of trying to protect me from the chafing and rashes that come with the heat and movement.

The summer before I left for college, a group of friends and I went to Cedar Point for the day, a theme park full of some of the world's tallest and fastest roller coasters. I wore a tank top and denim shorts I'd accidentally cut too short from a pair of jeans. I walked carefully all day, spending my time in lines leaning against the chains that separated the rows of people, my legs apart and not touching.

Andy begged me to ride Thunder Canyon, a water ride that sent you and a group of riders through a canyon-like river full of rapids and waterfalls. As a rule, I don't take water rides. The recycled water grosses me out, and I'm terrified of skin-eating bacteria. Also, my hair doesn't look great after it air-dries, and I don't have the type of body that does well walking long distances while wet. But against my better judgment I joined him, and at the end of the ride, I was soaked.

By the time I got home that night, the denim of my wet shorts had chafed my thighs bloody. My mom coated the open bumps with Neosporin and laid ice packs on each leg as I stretched beside her on the couch.

In the winter I try to keep my heavy body light on its feet, careful not to walk too forcefully or squat too quickly. I live in one perfect pair of jeans, fully aware that all my time inside of them is borrowed.

But then one afternoon I'm sitting in my car in the drive-through of a Sonic waiting for tots and a large cherry limeade, and I look down to see pink skin bubbling. I've buried more jeans than there are Batman movies.

Before I dispose of the cloth corpse, I rip off the button

above the zipper and toss it in a bowl in my top drawer the same way my roommate in college used to steal a sock, just one, from the men who slept over in our dorm room. Trophies of things we've devoured.

My thighs are cannibals.

I will never be the woman who can have sex in a shower stall or the front seat of a car. Those small spaces can't accommodate the wingspan necessary for my legs.

Da Vinci's *Vitruvian Man* wasn't art, it was an instruction manual for how to access my vagina.

Andy and I bought a king-size bed. I told him we needed it because he sleeps too close to me on a smaller mattress, and that sometimes he sleeps facing the same way I do, so his breath is touching my breath. I take it I don't need to explain anything further, jury of my peers.

What I love the most about the mattress is how much it dwarfs me. How small I feel lying on it, even when Andy is there beside me. And when he puts his hand on my hip because it's Friday night, or he likes the new dress I wore that day, or because our kids are at my mom's and we're living our lives as horny rabbits now, I don't get self-conscious, not then and not when he slides his hand between my legs after I turn to him on my side.

I don't make excuses, or adjust my body so that he doesn't have to push his hand through thick, weighted flesh to get to the center of me.

I spread across the large mattress and wait for Andy to climb into me. He is half my size, and when I wrap my legs around him, he disappears.

My thighs are Sirens.

"What are those lines, Mom?" Gigi asked, tracing the purple veins along my left thigh with her finger.

We stretched our legs out straight in front of us under the only tree at the playground. The boys played football in the field next to us, but Gigi was the only girl, and like me, she gets bored quickly playing by herself.

"They are varicose veins," I told her. "They are genetic, which means Oma also has them, and you might one day, too."

"I hope so." She sighed.

I only recently started wearing shorts. We were visiting Andy's parents in Florida, and this sweaty body can only take so much humidity before it starts to act irrationally. A couple margaritas later and I was either slaughtering a pair of jeans or shaving my head, and Andy didn't have his electric razor with him because he was growing a "vacation beard." I remember walking out of the bedroom in my newly cutoff shorts and Wyatt looking up from his game of Uno at the table with his grandmother to say, "Wait, they make shorts for moms, too?"

It was not an easy transition. There was chafing and insecurity and perfecting the "fat-girl sidestep." (You know that thing where you try to discreetly toss one of your legs off to the side midstride, hoping to create enough of an opening to allow for the bunched-up fabric to fall free of its own accord, self-correcting the shorts' ride-up predicament.)

I had been hiding my legs from the people who would have judged me the least. My kids see my thighs as part of the legs of their mother, the woman who cares for them and loves them and teaches them how to be in this world.

My husband sees them as soft flesh to consume whole or rest his hand on, unwavering in his love for me. You know, there is no box to check on a divorce form for dimpled thighs or stretch marks. The only love that threatens to end over cellulite is the love you offer to yourself.

I've decided to indulge these thighs. I let them walk around like banging thunder, and I feed them denim like gremlins after midnight.

I don't turn the lights off anymore. I don't hide them under maxis or jeans in 100 percent humidity. I'm no longer embarrassed about their dimples, veins, or stubble.

My thighs are shameless.

CHAPTER 12

Everything I Want to Say to My Daughter

When I look at her I'm envious. Envious that she figured out how to use the same body I was given but squandered for so long. I'm envious when she stands at the edge of the gymnastics mat, sucks all the air in the room into her lungs, and then charges toward the vault; her thick thighs are amazing muscular machines. I am envious that at age eight she is the most seen person in every room, and that she walks into a store and agrees to buy girls' size-10-plus shorts because they fit her legs better and that's that. No overanalyzing. No self-hate. No stages of body grief.

And that gap. Oh, the gap in her teeth brings me to my knees.

If I could take anything back in my life, it would be getting the gap between my two front teeth filled in.

"The bonding will last between five and ten years," the doctor told my mom as he gently filed smooth the new slim space between my teeth.

My friend Kristen had her teeth bonded in eighth grade, too, and I watched in horror as her bonding popped out whenever she bit into an apple or during a game of softball. And yet mine persisted.

My sophomore year of college, I went to see *Almost Famous* and I remember falling in love with Anna Paquin's character, Polexia Aphrodisia. Polexia had pouty lips, and pink heart-shaped sunglasses, and the most perfect gap between her two front teeth, just as I once had.

I made the decision that when this bonding finally fell out, I would not replace it. It's been twenty-three years, I've eaten hundreds of apples, and I'm still waiting.

Gigi will fill her gap in over my cold dead corpse.

"How do I help my daughter not hate her body?"

This is, hands down, the most frequent question women ask me. And I always know when it's about to happen, because a hand shoots up or a woman in line at a bookstore gets to the table, and I see the look on her face and I know exactly what she's about to say.

You know that moment right before you cry, the moment when you are afraid to blink because you know that if you close your eyes, the tears will rise up behind your eyelids, and when you open them again, the tears will splash down your face and they won't stop? That's the look.

I still see that look in the mirror sometimes, and I don't

expect it ever to go away, because children are hard and the world can be terrible.

I have the honor of speaking in junior highs and high schools about bullying, body image, and female empowerment. It always goes about the same way. I start off talking, telling the girls my story, showing them a couple of hideous school pictures from my youth, and then we break up into smaller groups to talk about ourselves. In one group, we talk about the things in our lives that make us feel strong and happy. In others, we talk about the people we look up to, and how we can emulate what we like in them. And then we talk about the crappy stuff. The times we hurt, the times we feel alone, all the things that take a little bit of our shine away from us. At the end of the day, everyone is raw and happy and hopeful. And I am, too.

But then I get into my car and I cry.

I cry because I know that at least half of those girls will go home, and every single step forward we took today will be undone by their parents.

It's hard to feel good about yourself when your mom makes you be her diet buddy. It's hard to like yourself when your father tells you he wishes you were more active. And it's almost impossible to raise kids who like themselves when you don't even like yourself.

My daughter, Gigi, is eight and has always been a bit eccentric in her fashion choices. She loves pairing colorful tights with patterned skirts, or shorts with tall boots. She throws her hair up into a messy bun and tops it with a bow.

And the girl can apply glitter eyeliner like a pro, while I walk out of the bathroom looking like a panda after trying to tackle a winged cat eye for an hour.

My sons, Wyatt and Jude, are ten and eleven, respectively, and I still pick out their outfits, which I am fine with, because at least I know they're wearing underwear and applying deodorant. I do the same for their father.

Whenever we go out, the boys rush through their pile of clothes, and then right before we are set to leave, I call for Gigi, who comes bounding down the stairway in something colorful and whimsical and ready for the world.

And then one day that stopped.

"Does this look okay?" she asked, leaning against the door of my bathroom, watching me do my makeup.

"You look awesome," I told her, meeting her eyes in the mirror.

And then she walked away, but not the way she usually walked, bouncing and confident and defiant. She looked suddenly very small and unsure of herself.

She came into my bathroom and asked me the same question the next day, and almost every day after that. I asked her all the important questions, whether something had happened at school, or if anyone had been mean to her. I wondered if there was something I had missed. I spoke to her teacher, studied the shows she was watching on the Disney Channel, texted with her friends' moms, and even took her to lunch to talk about how she felt about herself, and asked if there was anything she wanted to tell me. There wasn't.

"Does this look okay, Mom?" It just kept happening.

Gigi is stunning, and I know I'm supposed to say that because I'm her mom, but seriously, she's gorgeous. She has long dark hair, big brown eyes, and a dimple in her right cheek. I love every single inch of her, and in my eyes, she is perfect.

Not long after this, Andy got us tickets to see my favorite band, Hall & Oates. I should be embarrassed telling you that, but I'm not. I have a very real crush on Daryl Hall.

It was an outdoor concert, and I was feeling a bit frustrated with my summer outfit choices, the pile of discarded sundresses growing ever higher as I yanked one after the other off the hanger. I'd put it on, stare at myself in disgust, and then stomp into the bedroom in front of Andy.

"Does this look okay?" I asked again, sweaty and annoyed.

Ah, see? You see what I just said right there? Putting on an outfit and parading in front of Andy for approval had become so second nature I didn't even realize it was happening. And I didn't even want his approval. Andy has a terrible sense of fashion. If what he wore were up to him, he'd be wearing basketball jerseys with white T-shirts under them and gym shorts to dinner. I think I was just looking for him to be more excited about my body than I was feeling at that moment.

If I walked in and his eyes lit up and he told me I was stunning, maybe his enthusiasm about my outfit could carry me through the night knowing that I looked okay to everyone else, even if I didn't think so.

"Does this look okay, Mom?"

Yeah, Gigi learned that from me.

It's hard, as parents, to see ourselves as the potential villains in our kids' lives, especially since we spend so much time protecting them. We see our personal body insecurities and self-hate as affecting only us, when in reality, they play out like daylong soap operas in front of impressionable audiences. Kids aren't born with a narrative for how to treat themselves. We supply that, and we do it not only directly, but indirectly, in how we treat ourselves.

In this episode of How to Be a Woman, *Brittany asks her husband three times if she looks fat in her jeans and berates herself in the bathroom mirror before spending the next twenty minutes looking for God in front of an open refrigerator. Tune in next week when she cries in the dressing room at Target and then mumbles under her breath that the woman in front of her on line looks slutty in those shorts.*

Gigi was asking if her outfit looked okay because by watching me, she thought that was what women did. Women put things on and then ask other people if they look good. Our children learn to be adults from us, and sometimes our teaching methods just plain suck.

It's pretty pointless to try to talk Gigi into loving her body, when according to her own mother, the adult version is worthless and disgusting. So there's step one. **You want to teach your daughter how not to hate her body? Stop hating yours out loud.**

Obviously the goal is for you to learn to love yourself

entirely, but that is a long journey that can't be taken at the expense of your child. So right now, just shut up and pretend you like yourself. Save the diet talk, food shaming, and extreme body hate for an adult you can have constructive conversations with. Your daughter is not that adult.

Teach her how to enjoy dressing her body. This was an incredibly hard skill to learn as an adult. I spent most of my youth obsessing over everything I couldn't fit into; I never learned how to dress the body I had.

I hated to shop. When I was a kid, it was a lot of my mom shoving me into dressing rooms with armfuls of clothes she picked out for me and asking, "Well, does it fit?"

When I wish she had asked:

"Does this sweatshirt feel good on your skin?"

"Can you dance in these overalls?"

"Can you tell the obnoxious boy who sits behind you in math to shut up in this dress?"

"Do you like this skirt enough to have it featured in the slide show about your life that we show before your presidential inauguration?"

Gigi and I spend a lot of time shopping; in fact, it's our favorite activity. Fashion is a big part of my job, and I've always made sure to include her in the process of selecting clothes, putting together outfits, and creating the guides I share with my readers. There are a lot of scary things in this world; a bathing suit or a pair of jeans shouldn't be one of them. I don't ever want my daughter to dread dressing herself, or feel like her options are limited by the shape of her body.

Remind her that everyone has flaws. I remember when Charlie Hunnam was cast, temporarily, as Christian in *Fifty Shades of Grey,* and not being a *Sons of Anarchy* watcher, I had to google him. Every picture that came up showed this oiled and shirtless god of a man. He had messy blond hair, a scruffy beard, lots of muscles, and even that V thing that guys sometimes have near their groin that makes you pregnant when you look at it directly.

While he is obviously a very attractive man, I look at him and realize I can't relate to him at all. He doesn't even look like someone who'd be friends with me.

I always take comfort in watching eighties movies. They are like wool blankets I can wrap around me when I want to feel happy and included. I like watching them because the people who starred in them feel relatable.

Teeth weren't bleached white—heck, they weren't even straight, the bottom row all jumbled together and overlapping. Noses were big and disproportionate. And the boobs were either tiny, pointy, or like two heavy melons straining the bands of the actresses' bras. I look at those women and think that if I told them my nipples pointed down, they'd say, "Oh, girl, me too!"

The stars of eighties films aren't unattainable. They look like the girls I go to P.F. Chang's with when I find a babysitter or the guy whose eyes I knowingly meet when I'm looking for someone to commiserate with because the loser in front of us at McDonald's can't decide what he wants to order.

Would-be Christian Grey, Charlie Hunnam, was thirty-three years old when he was cast as Christian Grey. The same age as Steve Martin when he made *The Jerk*. I don't know anyone who looks like Charlie Hunnam. I know five guys who look like Steve Martin. Also, *The Jerk* is a classic. *Fifty Shades* is decidedly not.

Showing Gigi nothing but flawless celebrities not only sets the bar of self-esteem at insurmountable, it's also incredibly boring. I want to show her why scars, back fat, and lisps can be not only beautiful, but cool.

When I was thirteen I used to pray for my perfectly straight teeth to bend like Jewel's, because how could something with that much character not be extraordinary?

Teach her how to deal with self-hate. As much as I want to hide all my body hate moments and failures from Gigi, doing that will only handicap her when she faces them on her own. Teaching your daughter how to better handle those moments when she feels weak or worthless or unpretty will lessen the chance of them consuming her.

I make no secret about being a tourist in the land of loving my body. I do not fully understand the rituals or customs; I just try to fake the language enough that I am able to find a bathroom when I need one.

So when I get lost or frustrated, I try not to totally shelter my daughter. In fact, her presence keeps me safe, warning me to be gentler to myself in front of her. The same way Andy takes my phone away from me when I am drinking red wine because I'll only start drunk-texting all my contacts various Adele lyrics, Gigi keeps me respectable.

So she sees my down days, but more important, she sees that the sadness is only temporary. She sees me pick myself up and move forward, because these days, my body hate has a very short memory.

Show her how to be a better woman to other women. For the love of God, stop the cycle.

I believe women are born with an innate set of checks and balances. Like the government, only instead of ending wars or dictatorship, our system only works if it preserves a consistent level of self-esteem. When we see a woman who is heavier than us, or less conventionally attractive, feeling better about herself than we do, our checks and balances system is triggered, and we work to discredit and destroy her.

"If I feel like shit, everyone must feel like shit!"

We make passive-aggressive remarks about this woman, we plant seeds of doubt, and we settle into the safety net provided by the Internet to gossip in anonymity.

"What is with young girls today dressing like sluts?"

"This is why I only have guy friends, women are too dramatic."

"I just ran a 5k, cleaned the house, bathed all nine of my kids, and meal-prepped for the week. What's your excuse?"

Fat-shaming, mom-shaming, slut-shaming . . . look at all the types of shame we have! Men have none. We hide these attacks behind "no offense," "not to be mean but," and "sorry not sorry," but that only proves we're malicious. We are the perfect war machines, and the government should really just hand the entire military over to us women to shame Kim Jong-un into stepping down by talking about his bad eyebrows and the fact that he looks like a gerbil with a high fade.

We need to teach our daughters that their right to be treated respectfully is directly tied to the rights of the person they are shaming. To okay it for one okays it for all.

Dear Gigi,

Every year with you is my new favorite year. Even though soon I know the bubble that you and I hide inside will pop, and you'll have to relearn everything I've taught you in front of a much different and less forgiving audience.

When they tell you that you aren't enough, question their math. You come from a long family of women who are "too much." We are "too much" in personality, "too much" in quirks, and "too much" in thighs. But you will never be not enough.

When your jeans don't fit, buy a bigger pair. Larger jeans are worth the dinners with your best friends, the gelato during a semester in Italy, sleeping in on Sundays if you are tired, and a movie night on the couch with someone you love.

When they tell you that you are not like other girls,

do not thank them. Tell them that you are exactly like other girls; the ones who cry, and sing, and scream. Do not ever let them pit you against other girls.

Never apologize for your body. Ever.

And lastly, I fully expect that one day you'll stop believing me when I tell you you're beautiful. You'll plug your ears, and point to the world around you, and take every one of its harsh words over mine. My only hope is that it takes you thirty less years to realize I was right and they were wrong than it took me to figure out the truth for myself.

Mom

P.S. Promise me, Gigi, you will never fill that gap between your front teeth.

CHAPTER 13

I'm Not Sorry

Sometimes I feel like I was supposed to have been born an Olsen. Like the fourth one, the fat one who was super excited about her sisters' successes but had no interest in Hollywood and instead stayed home to raise chickens in her backyard. I say this because the boho gene is strong in me. I blame my Taurus roots pulling me toward all things flowy, earthy, and easy.

Plus, the loose fit of bohemian dresses and tops opens the door for me to shop in places that I might not otherwise fit into, which is how I found myself inside a store known for cheap and trendy women's clothing in stupidly small sizes. Eyeing their width, I grabbed a few flowy tops and headed to the fitting room, where the attendant smiled and took the hangers from my hand.

"Now, one of these is a crop top," she said, sifting through my selections and hanging them on the door of my stall.

It was both a statement and a question, and perhaps even a warning. But I just nodded and followed her into the dressing room. To be honest, I hadn't known it was a crop top, those aren't typically things I gravitate toward on account of being a little self-conscious about my weirdly deep belly button, and having no idea where someone my size or my age would even wear a crop top.

The crop top was cute, a black billowy tank top that sat just below the underwire of my bra cup. It felt easy and cool, a nice antidote to the summer heat. I had no idea what I'd pair it with off the top of my head, but it was only a few dollars, and I figured I could make it work.

Checking out, I was smiling as the man carefully folded up each item and placed it in the tiny paper bag. When he got to the black crop top he looked up and said, "So you know this is a crop top?" The same way I imagine a clerk at a fireworks store would warn someone buying M80s, "You know these explode when you light them, right?"

I did know that it was a crop top. I'd been reminded twice since I've walked into the store. I am not sure if those reminders were meant to dissuade me from buying an article of clothing for my body that has nothing to do with them, but in that moment, those reminders empowered me.

I wore that crop top to a concert with my husband. He stood behind me with his hands on my bare stomach, pulling me into him every few minutes to kiss the back of my head.

I wore that crop top to school pickup. Where the parents around me could have easily looked at me and decided I was no woman to be around their kids. Instead they high-fived me in the parking lot and complimented my PTA ideas.

I wore that crop top to the *Today* show, where I spoke with Kathie Lee and Elvis Duran about body image and its effects on women. I was the biggest person on that stage, and on my way up the steps to the studio the zipper on my skirt had broken open, and I still owned that look.

I wore that crop top and I was Cher. I was Scary Spice. I was Clarissa Explaining It All.

I started wearing that crop top out of spite, and then I bought five more because wearing them made me feel like a *woman* in a way not much plus-size clothing does. The crop tops reminded me that I was tired of hiding my body and pretending it was different from everyone else's.

I don't know a single person whose tummy doesn't fold in half when they sit down, and just because you can see mine in that crop top doesn't make it more true for me than it is for you. I won't hide my stomach to keep up some illusion that only thin bodies are beautiful. I am done wearing clothes to make other people feel comfortable at the expense of my womanhood.

We have entire generations of young girls who have no idea what their bodies are supposed to look like, because we only show them one kind, and hide the rest. We should be showing them that stomachs can roll, and stretch marks mean growth, that back fat happens to all women, and that belly buttons can sit high or low, in or out, shallow or as deep as Narnia.

This crop top normalized my body, not only to the world, but to me.

"Just so you know, this is a crop top," the tops said.

Well, I fucking hope so.

MY BODY IS NOT BRAVE

"You are so brave to wear that bikini, I could never do it."

I have the type of body that makes people call me brave when I wear a bathing suit. And the thing is, I think they think they're being nice when they say it, but if you really sit and think about it, it's pretty offensive.

It doesn't take an act of bravery for me to go swimming with everyone else. It takes an act of bravery to run into a burning building, or fly a fighter jet, or escape a war-torn country.

I'm just swimming in a pool, which is a pretty average activity. I'm probably not even swimming, but, rather, standing in a shallow area holding a drink, so really, I'm not even moving. Now, if that pool was full of water moccasins and I was rescuing a baby from the middle of it? Then yes, totally brave. Otherwise, just normal human stuff.

But one thing I don't want to do is discredit the huge mental feat it takes to wear a bathing suit, because that is very real for many women. When you hate your body, normal human activities become terrifying obstacles, especially when you see Internet memes making fun of overweight people, or magazines tearing apart perfectly toned celebrities.

Suddenly the most fearless thing you can do is put on a bathing suit, leave the house, and get into the water. Simply participating in life becomes an act of defiance under those circumstances.

Every November, Andy and I drive from northern Ohio to Florida to visit Andy's parents. I always remember road trips being tons of fun when I was a kid, but I've come to realize that that was because back then we didn't have to wear seat belts. My parents would take all the backseats out of our Dodge Caravan and my brother and I would build a giant fort in the middle of the van with all of our toys and pillows. It was like traveling in a ball pit. Now that everyone has to be in car seats and strapped in, their happiness hinging on Wi-Fi strength, road trips are boring and I hate them.

Andy's parents live in a rather infamous retirement community in central Florida. My kids enjoy the grandparent time and riding around the community in golf carts. I enjoy the 4 P.M. happy hour and being winked at by handsome old men in cargo shorts and white socks pulled up to their knees.

My kids love to swim, which is such a foreign concept to me. Even as a child, I dreaded wearing a bathing suit, and always looked for excuses to avoid putting one on during vacations or hotel stays. By contrast, my children can sniff out a neglected pool at even the seediest of roadside motels, and beg to take a dip at least once before bed.

Of the tens of pools available to residents at my in-laws' retirement community, only a handful are open to guests, especially guests with small children, which leads me to believe one thing: the pools we are welcome to use are definitely full of pee. There is nothing relaxing about being relegated to the family pool. Balls are being thrown across the length of the water, kids weighted down by swollen diapers are wading near the steps, and along the edge of the pool, moms holding iced coffees are chatting together while remaining focused on their broods.

And then there was me. I had packed only two two-piece suits for this vacation, both of them of the younger and sexier variety because we were spending the following week of our family vacation at the beach, where the standard of decency is a little more relaxed. I tried to rectify the situation by running to Walmart to buy a one-piece, but it was November, and Walmart wasn't selling bathing suits in November because it's winter, even though it's clearly still Satan's armpit in central Florida.

I decided on a lavender string bikini top with black high-rise bottoms, and then styled my hair in a ponytail meant to look messy and easy, despite taking over half an hour to do.

All the self-assurance I'd walked into the pool gate with

was squashed as I descended the steps into the pool and one of those iced-coffee moms muttered "yikes" under her breath. I don't know for sure that she was saying it in reference to me, but the timing was pretty dead-on, and the other three moms in similarly patterned tankinis looked my way as soon as she said it.

Maybe she thought my bathing suit was a little inappropriate for the family pool, and she'd have been right. Because as soon as I waded in, leaned against the four-foot-deep sign painted along the inner wall of the pool, and sank my body below the waves, my kids began to climb on me as if they've never been exposed to water before. Gigi clung to my neck and squealed and Wyatt attached his body to my right side, his legs wrapped around mine like a tiny kraken as I struggled to reposition the triangle of my bikini top back over my breast.

A woman getting into the pool with her tween daughter caught my eye. She wore a black athletic bikini and had actual ab muscles that flexed as she made her way deeper into the water. She spent a few minutes watching her daughter do handstands underwater, and then found some shade along the ledge beside me.

I worked to coax my children from my body, stuffing my boobs back into my lavender bikini top as they finally swam away, and met the woman's eye in the process and smiled. She made being a mom in a bathing suit with her kids look so cool. It was like watching a J.Crew ad unfold before my eyes. She could probably run after her daughter and not have to adjust her FUPA back into her bikini bottoms when she stopped.

"I hate the pool," she said, nodding toward me as she looked for her daughter.

"Me too," I squeaked, relieved that someone was talking to me.

"I don't even want to think about how much pee is in this thing, I just want to go back and put on my sweatpants." She sighed.

And that is when I realized we are all in this urine bath together. That nasty woman with the iced coffee probably would have been just as disgusted by me if I'd gotten into the pool wearing a wet suit. I wasn't there to impress forty-year-old moms. I was barely even there to impress my kids, and I had to hang out with them later. I was there to impress me. I'm the only one who needs to feel comfortable in my bathing suit, unless you're asking me if it's comfortable so you can borrow it, in which case the answer is no, because I don't like to share underwear with people.

Now, one thing that seems to get bantered about on the Internet quite frequently is this notion that "Fat girls shouldn't wear bikinis." It shows up in the comments section of my website often. As someone who has worn a bikini in Times Square, I can never quite wrap my head around it. A bathing suit is a bathing suit. My body shape doesn't change if my suit is a one-piece or two-piece. The only difference is that one suit is easier for me to pull down while going to pee.

And, if my being proud to show my body makes you want to get fat because you think I'm promoting obesity, or you think bikinis aren't flattering on plus-size women, well, guess what, I don't give a hoot. What about me wearing a bikini should make someone uncomfortable?

You know what makes me uncomfortable? Rattails. I was once behind a guy buying boiled peanuts in Macon, Georgia, and he had a rattail. I was going to say something to him about it, but then I remembered that he was a person with feelings and the right to personal choices, and I don't get to pick what made him feel attractive.

The reason it's so hard to imagine a world where you put on a bathing suit and walk around without ever worrying about how you look is that that world does not exist. Here's the reality of wearing a bathing suit in public: 99 percent of the people around you do not care how you look and won't say a word. The 1 percent who might, well, everyone already hates them anyways, because they're jerks. These are the people who hover over toilet seats in public bathrooms getting their pee all over everything and then don't wipe it up, or show up at weddings without RSVPing. *Nobody likes them.*

Does your bathing suit cover most of your bush?

Is there a screen print of Hitler on it?

All no's? Yeah, nobody cares, put the damn bathing suit on.

I'm going to wear my bikinis forever, into every urine-filled pool I find.

And I'm not sorry.

FOR THE FELLAS IN THE BACK

"I'm not sorry."

I find myself saying that a lot these days.

"I would never be able to pull that off," she says, eyeing me from the short hem of my sundress down to my extra-tall cork-wedge sandals.

"I'm not sorry."

"You'd be really pretty if you lost weight," the man at my nana's table said to me as I lunched with them at the nursing home.

"I'm not sorry."

"I'm selling a shake that could really change your life," she calls after me as I walk away from the bar at my friend Amanda's wedding reception.

"I'm not sorry."

"I don't think leggings are pants," she snarked into her coffee as she stood next to me on the sidelines of our sons' soccer game.

"I'm not sorry."

Here's the truth. I could be standing in front of you in a snowsuit, with a half-marathon medal around my neck, holding a laminated copy of my most recent blood work, EKG, and W-9 while running on a treadmill in a gym, and you'd still have contempt for this body. There is no win with you, society. And it can be pretty depressing. I mean, why even try?

But eventually I realized that if I consume so much of your day, if you can't do anything else with yourself when

I am around other than look at my body and decide if you like it or not, I don't want to hang out with you. You actually make me really uncomfortable.

I used to apologize for myself all the time. I've apologized to fitting room attendants in stores I don't feel 100 percent comfortable in. "I'm sorry, could I try this on?"

I've apologized to servers if my meal wasn't right, partially because I've seen the movie *Waiting* and I'm terrified to eat jizz, but also because I feel like my body is already so associated with food that if I say something, it will seem as if food is all I care about because I'm a giant fat food monster. "I'm sorry, I asked for steak on this salad, not salmon?"

I've done the shoulder-shrug, eyebrow-raise "I'm sorry" face to people who've had to sit next to me on airplanes, and I've apologized to a group of people that I had to squeeze in the middle of while a photograph for an award I won was taken. I was the winner. And I was the one apologizing. That doesn't even make sense.

Here's a list of things I will be apologizing for, going forward:

1. Farting in public.
2. Hitting an animal while driving. I live in the country, and squirrels are everywhere. I actually pull over, apologize profusely, and then give them their last rites, which is something you can totally google. It's a really nice ceremony. It's peaceful.

3. Watching *House of Cards* without you. I couldn't wait.

4. Accidentally hitting your car in a parking lot. Okay, seriously, how do I even have a license?

5. Forgetting your birthday.

6. Eating someone else's leftovers in the fridge. Put your stupid name on it, Andy!

What will I no longer be apologizing for? Everything else.

People talk about body love as a place you arrive at, with no mention of the journey it takes to get there. Like they just woke up with it one day, and how unfortunate for you that you haven't gotten there yet. Confidence is not something that just happens to you, like getting your first period or being selected for jury duty. It comes after spending years, decades even, putting in the hard work of getting to know your body, forgiving yourself for the way you've treated it, and learning to appreciate how absolutely amazing it is. That's why it feels so good when you finally figure this whole self-love thing out, and spaz out so much when it slips through your fingers every now and then. Body love is hard work.

Okay, new best friend, I hope you've enjoyed reading about my journey. I'm sorry if I made you cringe, or overshared about my sexy time or my underwear issues. I tend to talk a lot when I'm nervous. But maybe you learned a few things, too? I hope so. My wishes for you are as follows:

Do not ever worry that a love of fashion and self-care makes you any less of a card-carrying body-positive woman.

You deserve to be seen, so have fun with your experience and show the world who you are.

Please know that you can spend a whole lifetime losing and gaining weight, and none of it has a thing to do with who you are in your soul and mind; it only determines which pair of jeans you put on that day.

Always dress fearlessly. Explore new cuts, buy a bikini, give the middle finger to the snooty clerk selling you crop tops, and commit to at least three fashion mistakes and successes a month.

And lastly, know that this body is yours, and the limitations you put on it are your own, and subject to change without notice. No one gets to decide how much skin you show, or whether or not you shave your legs or wear a bra. Your standard of beauty is determined by you and you alone.

And for anyone who says our bodies make them uncomfortable?

We're not sorry.

CHAPTER 14

Thank-You Notes

Thank you, Natasha, for firing me from the Toledo Country Club, even though I had already quit a week prior, and you asked me to work until you returned from vacation to then fire me yourself. While being escorted out with my belongings was excessive and humiliating, the experience made me hungry to work harder to become wealthy enough to return to the country club as a member and treat you only half as badly as you treated me. Because twelve years later, I understand that it's hard to be a woman in a male-driven workplace and the only power you had is what you could exert over me. The only thing I have left to say to you is to ask you where you bought your amazing black power suits.

Thank you to my daughter's friend Genevieve, who

told me I looked "very fancy" when I volunteered as lunch mom. Your comment made me feel very confident that day, and I think of you every time I help one of my kids put a straw into their Capri Suns.

Thank you, Ashley Graham. Every time you wear a bathing suit cut high in the thigh, you blow my mind and make me damn proud to be a curvy woman in this world. Never stop doing it because I'm pretty sure I'm not the only woman you make feel that way.

Thank you to the man in Mexico who mistook me for a prostitute while I was waiting for the taxi I'd called. I wasn't sure how much I would charge should I ever become a sex worker, and now I know I was grossly undervaluing myself.

Thank you, Junior High Burn Book, for letting me know that I was ugly and that I "tried too hard" to get people to like me. That was a totally fair assessment of my teen years. I was that girl in school trying to give people gifts in exchange for friendship. Luckily, it seems as an adult I've simply run out of fucks to give.

Thank you, Mom, for being one of my best friends. Not many girls my age had great relationships with their mothers, but ours was always the exception. You were never a regular mom, you were a cool mom. I hope to have the same wonderful bond with my own daughter, until she slams the door in my face and tells me she hates me. Please call her and tell her what a great mom I really am when that happens.

Thank you to whoever invented the menstrual cup. It's

horrifyingly messy, but it's nice not waking up after a night of drinking and finding three tampons shoved up inside of me. You save me from toxic shock syndrome, and I appreciate that about you.

Thank you to the boy who told me I was really bad at giving blow jobs. You were right, I'm terrible. I can't seem to sync up my mouth with my hand around the shaft, and I never know what to do with my second hand. Do I play with the balls? Anyways, I'm certain my husband appreciates your honesty.

Thank you to Lucille Ball. You were the original "bitches get shit done" gal and may we not only share the roots on our heads, but persistence in being particularly loud and commanding in a man's world.

Thank you, ex–Lululemon CEO Chip Wilson and former Abercrombie CEO Mike Jeffries, for being massive dicks. You callously misjudged plus-size shoppers who were eager to shove money at your brands. It stung at first, but somehow we've managed to carry on without buying see-through athletic leisure or obnoxious graphic surfer T-shirts from either of your stores.

Thank you, Bill, who left me in the middle of homecoming to go home with his ex-girlfriend, Nikki. I ended up having an amazing night with my girlfriends. I was unsure about going to the dance with you in the first place because your eyes were always bloodshot and you smelled like rubber tires. It turns out my instincts were correct, and since then I've listened to them more.

Thank you to Mindy Kaling, for your impeccable execution in the wearing of short skirts, curvy thighs, and lighting-quick wit. I won't say I want to be you when I grow up, because I think we're the same age and that's condescending, so let's just settle for being long-distance best friends who text each other during *The Bachelorette*.

Thank you, Christian Siriano, for your inclusivity and wicked plus-size designs. Thank you for stepping up to the plate and dressing the amazing curvy women who are shunned by other designers. May I one day find myself in one of your gorgeous gowns, whether it be on the red carpet or while having a dance party in my backyard with my daughter.

Thank you, Internet trolls, for faking concern about my health in order to shame me about my body. Congratulations on still not being medical doctors *or* decent human beings. I'm sure everyone at your twenty-year high school reunion is going to be super-impressed by you.

Thank you to the Academy for this Oscar for Best Original Screenplay, and to Aidy Bryant, who portrayed me flawlessly.

Thank you, Mr. Green, my twelfth-grade English teacher. You are very hard to find. I sent identical handwritten letters to every "Mike Green" in the local phone book. I hope you got one. If not, I just wanted to say thank you for telling me that I would be an idiot to be anything in this world other than a writer. That has actually worked out really well for me.

Thank you, People of Walmart, for turning public humiliation into a sport. May you and your children never fall victim to the despicable hate you perpetuate for clicks and shares.

Thank you to every boy who would only make out with me in secret. In the moment, you made me feel special, but as I look back, you illustrated the shame you felt about dating someone who looked like me. Because of you, I never dated a boy who was embarrassed about what I looked like again.

Thank you, Andy, for being oblivious as to what size my jeans are. Some days it's all I can think about, and I try to show you what the tag says, but you simply don't care. Instead you spend the next thirty minutes worshiping my body enough for the both of us, and I forget what was on the stupid tag to begin with.

Thank you, Wyatt, for writing in your first-grade school report that you loved me because I had the softest belly, because I never cook in the kitchen, and because I sing really loud when I drink wine. This statement was so profoundly accurate that I've added it to my LinkedIn profile.

Thank you to my readers and followers. You have lined the journey of learning to love myself with companionship and support. I've definitely spent more time half-naked in public than I assumed I would have at this point in my life, but I wouldn't take back a minute. May we continue to lift each other up, overshare our bodies, and eat our feelings together for a long, long time to come.

ACKNOWLEDGMENTS

I am writing these acknowledgments while sitting next to my husband on the couch. Every time he tries to look over at my screen, I lean forward and cover it with my whole body. I think he thinks I am watching porn.

I wasn't watching porn, Andy. I was writing this thank-you to you. You've been my dedicated other partner for as long as I have written words, even though a solid half of them were about you. Thank you for being a willing participant in this life, for being the man I love more than anything, and for allowing me to check out of adult responsibility every few months to follow this dream.

Thank you to my kids: Jude, Wyatt, and Gigi. Thank you for always being my biggest cheerleaders, just as I am honored to always be yours. Even when you're teenagers and you tell me I'm embarrassing. I won't stop. Ever.

Mom and Dad, I know I don't say it enough, but I am so happy to have been raised by you, to have a life filled with stories and magic. I am so lucky to have you both.

Thank you to my editor, Carrie Thornton, for letting me write more books. I would be honored to write a thousand more for you, friend.

Kate McKean. You are an amazing friend and an amazing agent. Thank you for always answering my panicked texts and emails. I only feel competent because you remind me that I am when I need it the most.

I am very thankful to be surrounded by women who support me, who let me lean on them, and who have truly become my greatest family. Jodi, Jess, Laura, Sarah, Kelly, Melanie, Catherine, Heather, Robyn, Rhonda, Danielle, DaNetra, Shauna, and Jenelle, thank you for always leading by example and being the strong women in my life. I learn so much from you.

Rachel Smith, the only reason this book is finished is because you showed up at my house and made me finish it.

Thank you to Meredith Soleau, one of my most brilliant creative partners. Thank you for never saying no to any of my ideas, Mere.

And lastly, thank you to my Curvy Girl Community. You are the best sisterhood any girl could ever hope for.

Brittany Gibbons is a humorist, Internet personality, and nationally recognized positive-body-image advocate. She is the author of the *New York Times* best seller *Fat Girl Walking: Sex, Food, Love, and Being Comfortable in Your Skin . . . Every Inch of It* and writes the award-winning humor blog BrittanyHerself .com, which receives over 500k views a month. Brittany also founded the women's lifestyle magazine CurvyGirlGuide .com. She gave a 2011 TED talk on the reinvention of beauty and she's been the face of numerous fashion campaigns. Brittany's writing has been featured in the *New York Times*, *Huffington Post*, *Redbook*, *Woman's Day*, *Marie Claire*, *L.A. Times*, *The Stir*, and *Babble*, among many others. Brittany also hosts a weekly Google talk show called *Last Call Brittany* and the weekly podcast Girl's Girls. Brittany lives in Ohio with her husband and three children.